PORTLAND HEAD LIGHT & FORT WILLIAMS

Best Wishes to
Dick Wilson

Ken Thompson

PORTLAND HEAD LIGHT & FORT WILLIAMS

An Illustrated History With A Walking Guide Map

Kenneth E. Thompson Jr.

Kenneth E. Thompson Jr.

The Thompson Group
Portland, Maine

©1998, Kenneth E. Thompson Jr

The Thompson Group
55 Vannah Avenue
PO Box 3897
Portland ME 04104-3897

All rights reserved. No part of this publication may be reproduced, stored in a retrieval system, or transmitted in any form or by any means, including electronic, mechanical, photographic, or magnetic,

ISBN 0-9677650-0-5

Front Cover: Battery DeHart (1973) before it was buried, with Portland Head Light beyond, courtesy of the *Portland Press Herald*.
Frontispiece: In July of 1987 a field gun is fired at Fort Williams at the conclusion of the Portland Symphony Orchestra's rendition of *The William Tell Overture,* courtesy of *Chris C. Church / Portland Press Herald*.
Back Cover: Cannon, courtesy of *Chris C. Church / Portland Press Herald* and Battery Blair, *Portland Press Herald*.
Unless otherwise credited, photographs are those in the author's collection.

1999 marks the 100th Anniversary of the naming of Fort Williams.

Kenneth E. Thompson Jr. (1946-   ); BA, BS, MS Ed, University of Southern Maine; Assistant Historian 1970-71, United States Army Forces Southern Command, Fort Amador, Canal Zone; Assistant Director 1970-71, USARSO Museum, Fort Amador, Canal Zone; Historical Consultant 1988-92 to Island Institute, Rockland, Maine in the successful effort to save Fort McKinley's gun batteries.

Printed in the United States of America

DEDICATION

To my wife and children,
Jane Amanda (Brooks) Thompson
Stephen Frye Thompson
Amanda Jane Thompson

*Who have visited more forts
than they care to remember*

Acknowledgements

The author would like to extend
special thanks for their important contributions to:

Joel W. Eastman
Mason Philip Smith
Cape Elizabeth Historical Society

The author would also like to thank
the following individuals and
organizations whose resources or assistance
have been invaluable:

Ernest T. Bagley, Sr.
William David Barry
Jane B. Beckwith
Chris C. Church
Roger W. Davis
Thomas L. Gaffney
Harry L. Hardy
Janet S. Hill
Alex M. Holder, Jr.
Jayne A. Jordan
William B. Jordan, Jr.
Bruce L. Kempton
Nelson H. Lawry

Robert C. Malley
Michael K. McGovern
Constance C. Murray
Andrea R. Nemitz
Cheryl L. Parker
Al J. Ward

Cape Elizabeth Public Works Department
Greeley's Mills Cartography
Maine Historical Society
The Museum At Portland Head Light
Portland Press Herald
The Portland Room, Portland Public Library
The Provincial Press
South Portland-Cape Elizabeth Historical Society
Thomas Memorial Library, Cape Elizabeth

CONTENTS

Introduction	1
Portland Head, Cape Elizabeth, Maine	2
Portland Head, American Revolution	3
Portland Head Light	3
Portland Harbor Defenses, 1794-1861	11
Portland Head, 1862-1876	13
Cape Elizabeth, 1890s	15
Modern Defenses and Portland Head, 1891-1898	17
Fort Williams, 1899-1916	23
Fort Williams, World War I	41
Fort Williams, Between the Wars	44
Fort Williams and Portland Harbor, 1939-1941	57
Fort Williams and Portland Harbor, 1941-1943	70
Fort Williams and Portland Harbor, 1944-1945	84
Fort Williams, 1946-1963	88
Fort Williams Park	91
Bibliography and Further Reading Guide	94
Index	99
Walking Guide Map	*Inside the back cover*

Introduction

Symbolizing the rockbound coast of Maine, the lighthouse at Portland Head, officially designated Portland Head Light, has aided mariners for over 200 years. For seven decades starting in the 1890s, this lighthouse shared its scenic location with a large seacoast defense fortification, Fort Williams, a key element in the harbor defenses of Portland, Maine. While the fort has long passed into history, the lighthouse continues to function in the same role envisioned by its builders.

America's foremost 19th century poet, Henry Wadsworth Longfellow (1807-1882) was an occasional visitor to Portland Head Light during his youth in his native Portland, as well as later in adulthood. In November 1849 he wrote a poem, *The Lighthouse* (supposedly based on fond memories of the imposing beacon visible from Portland's Munjoy Hill), which began:

> The rocky ledge runs far into the sea,
>   And on its outer point, some miles away,
> The Lighthouse lifts its massive masonry,
>   A pillar of fire by night, of cloud by day.
>
> Even at this distance I can see the tides,
>   Upheaving, break unheard along its base,
> A speechless wrath, that rises and subsides
>   In the white lip and tremor of the face.
>
> And as the evening darkens, lo! how bright,
>   Through the deep purple of the twilight air,
> Beams forth the sudden radiance of its light
>   With strange, unearthly splendor in the glare!

Left: Fort Williams in 1964 looking northwest, with Portland Head Light at lower right. *Portland Press Herald*

Not one alone; from each projecting cape
   And perilous reef along the ocean's verge,
Starts into life a dim, gigantic shape,
   Holding its lantern o'er the restless surge.

PORTLAND HEAD, CAPE ELIZABETH, MAINE

Originally called Portland Point in colonial times, Portland Head is a rocky headland marking the southern extent of Casco Bay. The headland juts into the ocean at the entrance of Portland Sound, the main channel into Portland Harbor and the city of Portland three miles away.

To the confusion of many, Portland Head is in the town of Cape Elizabeth, not in its namesake city of Portland. This headland is three miles north of a larger headland named Cape Elizabeth by the Prince of Wales (later King Charles I of England) for his sister, first noted on a map printed by the famed adventurer Captain John Smith (of Pocahontas fame) in 1614 after returning from explorations in New England.

Princess Elizabeth (1596-1662) was the only daughter of King James VI of Scotland who became King James I of England in 1603, succeeding his grandfather's first cousin, Queen Elizabeth I. However, the two countries retained their separate identities and parliaments under a common ruler until 1707, when a political union with one parliament was formed as Great Britain.

Meanwhile, Princess Elizabeth had married a German prince, became Queen of Bohemia, and was the grandmother of an Elector (king) of Hanover who succeeded to the throne of England as King George I in 1714 on the death of his second cousin Queen Anne, who died without heirs. Since that time Elizabeth's descendants have included at least fifty-five European monarchs, including Frederick the Great, George III of England, Kaiser Wilhelm II, Czar Nicholas II, and all seven of the current occupants of the major European thrones.

Originally Portland and Cape Elizabeth were part of the town of Falmouth. When the southern portion of Falmouth was incorporated as a separate district in 1765 and as a town in 1775, it was assigned the name of the large headland, Cape

Elizabeth, by the legislature although the name Portland was the local choice.

The name Portland had been first applied to the smaller headland, the large island opposite (now Cushing Island), and the channel of water connecting the ocean to Falmouth Harbor sometime in the last half of the 17th century. When the peninsula portion of Falmouth became a separate town in 1786, that new town adopted the name Portland in honor of the nearby channel and headland with legislative approval. And, the name of the harbor was also changed from Falmouth to Portland.

PORTLAND HEAD, AMERICAN REVOLUTION

In the aftermath of the near total destruction (400 structures) of the densely settled peninsula portion of Falmouth by a British Navy flotilla under Captain Henry Mowatt on 18 October 1775, several militia earthwork fortifications were erected at various locations. One fort was at Spring Point in Cape Elizabeth, now part of South Portland, at the inner end of Portland Sound two miles north of Portland Point.

A guard of one non-commissioned officer and seven privates was established at Portland Point by May 1776 to watch for ships and to fire a cannon as an alarm for the fort at Spring Point, ultimately named Fort Hancock. However, having done its damage to Falmouth, the British Navy did not molest the town again during the American Revolution.

PORTLAND HEAD LIGHT

Agitation by local seafarers and businessmen for construction of a lighthouse at Portland Point began in 1785. The Mass-achusetts legislature (Maine was part of Massachusetts until 1820) authorized construction of a fifty-eight foot tower two years later to be built of rubble-stone and lime. The tower was twenty-four feet in diameter at its base, tapering as it rose. After the tower was nearly finished, local authorities discovered that a nearby headland would block the view of the light at sea, and determined that additional height was needed.

The legislature declined to appropriate more funds, but the U. S. Congress authorized additional expenditures in 1790 to

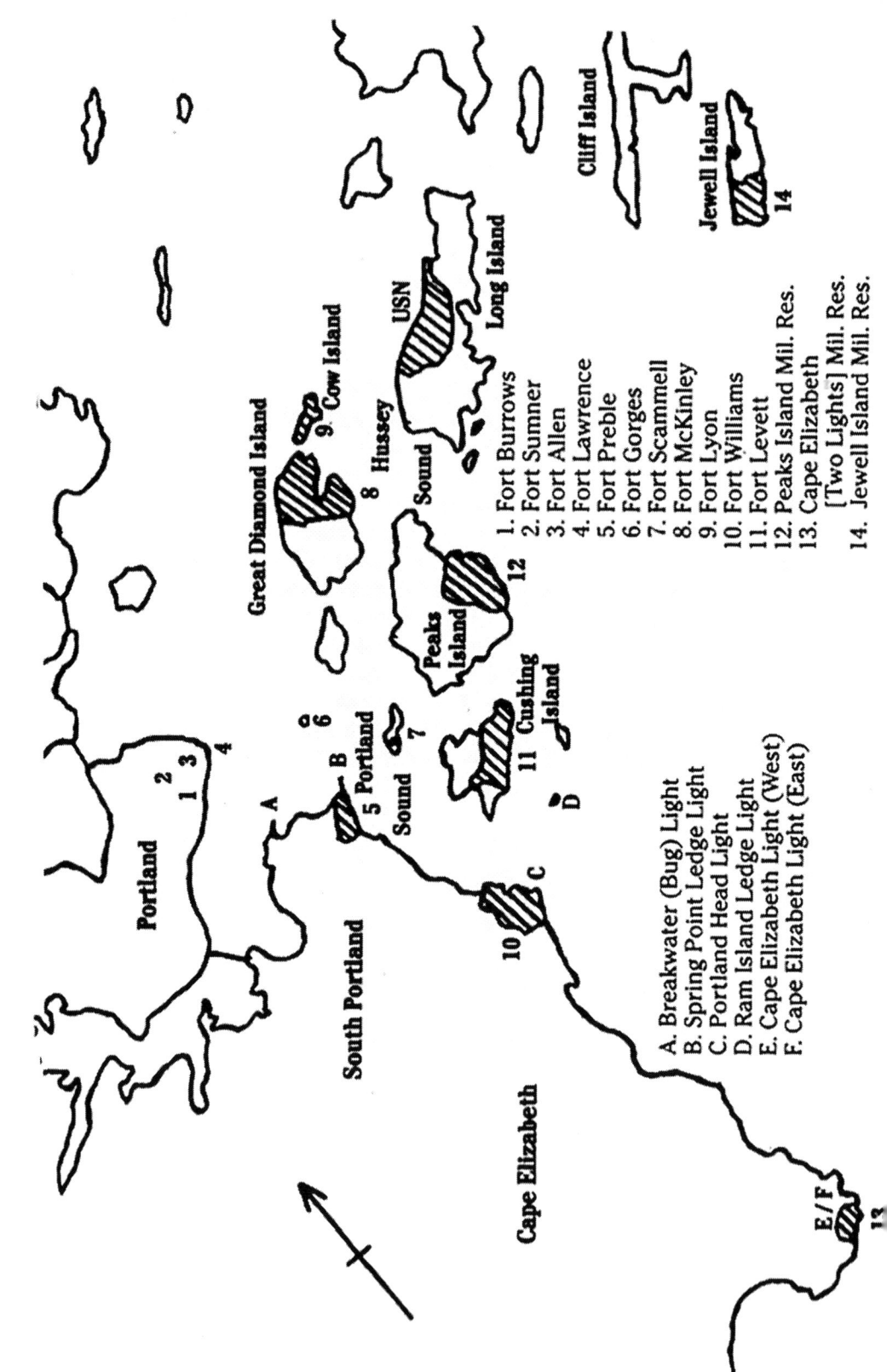

William B. Jordan, Jr.

Portland Head Light in 1883-84.

complete the project. When the additional fourteen feet were added to the sloping tower, the ten foot diameter at the top of the lighthouse was not wide enough to install the intended lantern. Authorities procured and installed a smaller lantern, and the tower was first lighted on 10 January 1791 with sixteen lamps of whale oil. President George Washington signed the commission of the first civilian lighthouse keeper. The lighthouse was under the supervision of the Bureau of Lighthouses, an agency established in 1789 as part of the Treasury Department (moved to the Commerce Department in 1903).

Portland Head Light was the first of six lighthouses in close proximity marking various points at the southern end of Casco Bay, with four still in operation. In 1828 two stone lighthouses were constructed at Dyer's Cove, Cape Elizabeth, four miles south of Portland Head. Formally known as the Cape Elizabeth Lights, the two structures were rebuilt in cast iron in 1874. While the west lighthouse was abandoned in 1924, the area has retained the name Two Lights.

The Breakwater Light (commonly called Bug Light) was constructed of wood in 1855 on the end of an earlier granite breakwater at Stanford's Point opposite the city of Portland, three miles north of Portland Head. Reconstructed of cast iron in 1875, it was abandoned in 1943. In 1897 the Spring Point Ledge Light was built on a ledge a few hundred yards offshore at Spring Point, a mile south of Stanford's Point and two miles north of Portland Head; in 1951 a granite breakwater was built connecting the lighthouse to Spring Point. In 1905 the Ram Island Ledge Light was built on an exposed ledge a mile and a half northeast of Portland Head.

In addition, five successive lightships were anchored over five miles southeast of Cape Elizabeth from 1903 until replacement by a Large Navigational Buoy (LNB) in 1975. The lightship was named *Cape Elizabeth* until 1913, when it was renamed *Portland*.

Portland Head Light was little changed from 1791 until the tower was reduced about twenty feet in height in 1813, and a small two-room keeper's quarters was constructed of stone in 1816. New reflectors were added to the light in 1850, and a new Fresnel lens was installed in 1855. The 4th order lens was almost twenty inches in diameter and two feet four inches in height. In that latter year, the tower was also lined in brick, and a wood-frame bell tower was built to support a 1500 pound fog bell.

In 1864 the tower was increased to its original height, and the light was upgraded with a 2nd order lens. The new lens was over fifty-five inches in diameter, and six feet one inch in height (now on display in the museum). At that time the light was first illuminated with kerosene. An ell was built connecting the lighthouse and the quarters by 1864, and a second story was added to the quarters in 1870. In 1869 the bell tower was destroyed in a gale, and a new pyramidal tower was built the following year to house a new 2000 pound bell. However, the new bell was replaced after two years by a Daboll trumpet placed on top of the wooden engine house.

After Halfway Rock Light was built in 1871 in outer Casco Bay, the Lighthouse Board (the renamed Bureau) recommended

Cape Elizabeth Historical Society
Portland Head Light in 1885-90.

that Portland Head Light be relegated to a smaller 4th order light, and again reduced twenty feet in height. The classification of the light was changed from a headland light, a primary aid to navigation, to that of a harbor light. The reduction was made in 1883, but local mariners convinced the influential Maine congressional delegation of the folly of that decision. The 2nd order light was restored two years later, as was the height to its present seventy-two feet, and the light could be seen seventeen miles at sea.

On the night of 24 December 1886, the captain of the bark *Annie C. Maguire* arriving from Buenos Aires lost his bearings, and caused his ship to wreck on the ledge only yards south of the lighthouse. All hands were saved with the assistance of the lighthouse keeper and his family, but the ship was smashed to bits by the surf caused by a powerful storm a week later.

The small keeper's house was removed from the site and relocated as a private home in the Cape Cottage neighborhood in 1890, and a large wood house was built early the next year to accommodate two families. After 1893 the lighthouse complex had to share the headland with massive gun batteries of what would become Fort Williams.

The light was extinguished for several weeks in the early part of the Spanish-American War until it became apparent that the Spanish Navy posed no threat. Similarly, the light was little affected by World War I. Initial fears were quickly dispelled, since the German Navy posed no threat to the American seacoast by the time of United States entry in the war in April 1917.

In 1928 the kerosene lamp inside the Fresnel lens was replaced by a 500-watt electric incandescent bulb with 32,000 candlepower, and the light was changed from a fixed to a flashing signal for the first time. In 1938 an air diaphragm chime horn replaced the Daboll trumpet installed in 1872.

In 1939 the Bureau of Lighthouses (which had been renamed the Lighthouse Board during the period 1852-1910) was merged into the U.S. Coast Guard, but the civilian keepers were retained until they retired. From 1791 to 1946, fifteen civilians had been appointed as keepers of Portland Head Light, including four men with twenty or more years, and two sets of father and son: Barzillai Delano served 1796-1820, Joshua Freeman 1821-1840, James Delano 1854-1861, Joshua Strout 1869-1904,

Annie C. Maguire **wrecked at Portland Head 24 December 1886.**

and Joseph W. Strout 1904-1928. The Strout family combined for fifty-nine consecutive years of service, with Joshua's wife Mary and son Joseph serving as assistant keepers during his long stint.

Joseph W. Strout and his bird house model of Portland Head Light.

The Coast Guard had been formed in 1915 by the consolidation of two other bureaus in the Treasury Department: the Revenue Cutter Service (1790) and the Life-Saving Service (1871). Sumner I. Kimball (1834-1923), a Maine native and Bowdoin College graduate, had established the latter service in 1871, and headed the organization until it was absorbed into the Coast Guard forty-four years later. A Life-Saving Station was maintained at Dyer's Cove near the two Cape Elizabeth Lights from 1887 to 1964. Also, a Buoy Station has been maintained in Portland Harbor since before the Civil War, first at House Island, then Little Diamond Island, and continuing to the present at South Portland.

During World War II the Navy assumed control over the Coast Guard, and extinguished Portland Head Light from 5 June 1942 until 29 June 1945 as part of the Dimout Program as well as to deny the enemy a reference point for the entrance to Portland Harbor and the defenses of Fort Williams. In 1946 the first coast guardsmen replaced the last civilian appointee of the Bureau of Lighthouses as keepers of Portland Head Light.

In 1958 a rotating beacon emitting two beams of light 180° apart replaced the Fresnel lens. During a fierce storm in April 1975 huge waves broke through the seaward wall of the 1888 engine house destroying the fog warning system and knocking out the power, extinguishing the light. The beacon was quickly restored, and a temporary foghorn system was installed until another structure could be built to house a new system.

In 1989 the Coast Guard automated the light as part of its nationwide automation program. Formal decommissioning occurred on 7 August as the Coast Guard withdrew the keepers,

Jane A.B. Thompson
Portland Head Light with winter surf.

and turned the quarters over to the town of Cape Elizabeth for a proposed museum. The Coast Guard retained control over the light, the sound signals, and other navigational aids at the site. Located at Longitude 43° 37.4' N and Latitude 70° 12.5' W, the modern light can be seen twenty-four miles at sea.

Since the late 1980s, Portland Head Light has stood as a welcoming sentinel on several occasions to Portland Harbor visits by two of the most impressive vessels plying the high seas: the nuclear-powered aircraft carrier USS *John F. Kennedy* and the graceful passenger liner *Queen Elizabeth 2*.

On 20 September 1992 The Museum at Portland Head Light was dedicated. Occupying the first floor of the keepers' quarters, the museum has four rooms depicting the history of the lighthouse, including models of the structure at its various stages. One room illustrates the military presence, with many photographs and a large model of Fort Williams.

Listed on the National Register of Historic Places, Portland Head Light has long been considered one of the most picturesque, painted, and photographed sites in the United States. Noted Portland seascape artist George M. Hathaway (1852-1903) painted different views of the lighthouse. His views were so realistic and popular that they were reproduced in color in large quantities on pre-World War I, German-printed, picture postcards distributed by the George W. Morris Publishing Company of Portland, one of the earliest and largest distributors of picture postcards in the country.

In 1927 the famous American artist Edward Hopper (1882-1967) painted two watercolors of the lighthouse, now hanging in public galleries in Boston and Hartford. In 1981 the Postal Service issued an 18-cent coil stamp (Scott #1891) showing the American flag and Portland Head Light. And, in 1990 the Postal Service issued a stamp booklet of five different 25-cent lighthouse stamps (Scott #2470-2474). Although not depicted on any of the stamps, the tower of Portland Head Light was pictured on the booklet cover, as well as on the official USPS souvenir card. The lighthouse remains a popular subject for postcards, calendars, and personal checks, often published and available far beyond Maine.

One final note is in order. In addition to the confusion over the fact that the Portland Head Light is not in the city of Portland, the name of the lighthouse is occasionally misspelled. The name is sometimes seen as Portland Headlight. Headlights are for automobiles, not as a class of lighthouses located on headlands.

PORTLAND HARBOR DEFENSES, 1794-1861

The United States Army began to fortify the major harbors from Portland to St. Mary's, Georgia in 1794. The closest major American harbor to Europe, Portland was an important trading port with an excellent deep-water harbor. While Portland Head did not enter the picture until 1862, a fort was built on Munjoy Hill in Portland as the harbor's only defense, named Fort Sumner.

In the aftermath of the embargo and crisis of 1807, the government began construction of a series of forts from Eastport, Maine to New Orleans, Louisiana in 1808. Two new earth and masonry forts were built to cross fire on opposite sides of the inner end of Portland Sound: Fort Preble on the site of Fort Hancock, and Fort Scammell on House Island. The name of the latter fort is more often, but not exclusively, spelled Scammel by the Army, yet it was originally named by Secretary of War Henry Dearborn (as was his son) for Colonel Alexander Scammell of American Revolution fame.

The state of Massachusetts also built three militia earthworks on the Portland peninsula late in the War of 1812 to supplement the three federal forts: Fort Burrows (1813), Fort Lawrence (1814), and Fort Allen (1814), all named for contemporary naval heroes. The latter fort survives on Munjoy Hill, and can faintly be seen from Portland Head. These forts mounted cannon which had an effective range of about one mile. Although the British Army maintained large bases in Eastern Maine at Castine and Eastport, and the British Navy lurked off Casco Bay during the War of 1812, the Portland forts proved an able deterrent to British invasion.

On 5 September 1813 a furious naval battle between the USS *Enterprise* and the HMS *Boxer* took place thirty miles east of Portland Head and about four miles south of Pemaquid. The *Enterprise* scored a decisive victory, and returned to Portland Harbor the next morning with the captured prize and its crew, as well as the bodies of the two slain ship captains. The two ships passed Portland Head Light and anchored off Fort Preble since they were not able to navigate against the outgoing tide in their damaged conditions. The ships docked in Portland on the afternoon incoming tide, and the two captains were buried side by side in Eastern Cemetery, where their tombs may be seen today.

After 1817 the government began an ambitious program to construct massive, multiple-tiered, masonry forts to replace the small, outdated defenses of 1808. These forts were designed in tiers to increase the firepower against enemy ships. For the next five decades, many fortifications were proposed, fewer planned, and an even lesser number actually funded and built, as evaluations periodically changed. Projects were grouped in three different classes based on the urgency of construction.

A substantial fort at Portland, probably at Fort Preble, was proposed in the 1821 report of the Board of Engineers for construction in the second period. In the 1826 report, a new Fort Preble was joined by a new Fort Scammell on House Island among the proposed sites in the second phase, while a proposed fortification on Hog Island Ledge was on the list for the third phase. In 1836 a new Fort Preble was advanced to the first phase, while House Island and Hog Island Ledge remained in the second and third phases, respectively. However, no new masonry construction was begun in Portland Harbor until the late 1850s.

Existing forts Preble and Scammell were among a large group of forts that were maintained until new construction was initiated. While awaiting eventual replacement, these two outdated forts received additional guns mounted in exterior earthen batteries in the 1840s. A number of guns mounted behind an earth wall was called a battery as opposed to a more sophisticated, enclosed fort.

In 1851 the proposed projects at House Island and Fort Preble were swapped in priority, while Hog Island Ledge remained in the third stage. Yet, when the first masonry fort was begun in Portland Harbor in 1858, it was built on the latter site. A three-tiered Fort Gorges was designed to mount ninety–five guns, which would cross fire with those of forts Preble and Scammell. Just before the Civil War, work began on a new three-tiered Fort Preble at Spring Point. These new fortifications would mount cannon with an effective range of about three miles.

PORTLAND HEAD, 1862-1876

With the outbreak of the Civil War, substantial masonry modifications to Fort Scammell were also begun. In January 1862 the Corps of Engineers drafted plans for smaller earthwork batteries at seven other locations to supplement the unfinished masonry forts, including a six-gun battery at Portland Head, but none of these batteries were built.

In June 1863 Portland Head was a passive spectator to a daring Confederate Navy raid into Portland Harbor. Lieutenant Charles W. Read, CSN, and his two-dozen man crew boldly sailed into the harbor on the evening of 26 June past Portland Head Light, the unfinished forts, and the garrison at Fort Preble.

Shortly after midnight the raiders seized the USRC *Caleb Cushing,* a sailing ship of the Revenue Cutter Service. Fleeing the harbor under cover of darkness through Hussey Sound, the unlucky Confederates encountered a light breeze. Portlanders swiftly assembled a force of civilians and soldiers aboard steamships after daybreak to pursue the raiders. The pursuers caught up to the *Caleb Cushing* about twelve miles east of Portland Head, and the Confederate raiders abandoned the ship to the torch, which succeeded in blowing up the ship. The raiders were retrieved by the motley fleet, which steamed back to Portland past Portland Head. The prisoners were held at Fort Preble until transferred to Fort Warren in Boston Harbor in July.

In 1864 plans were prepared for a large, two-tiered masonry fort at Portland Head similar to Fort Gorges, but the war ended before these plans were executed. In fact, the development of rifled cannon during the Civil War made the masonry forts obsolete, and all construction ceased by the early 1870s, leaving forts Gorges and Scammell nearly complete and new Fort Preble only partially begun.

Prior to the Civil War, the majority of cannon were smoothbore, firing spherical cannonballs. The war provided optimum testing of newer cannon with rifling (grooves) in the barrel which could fire an elongated, pointed projectile with far greater accuracy and effect, since the trajectory of the projectile could be stabilized and the wind resistance lessened.

The breaching of the eight-foot thick brick walls of Fort Pulaski in Georgia by Union artillery in April 1862, as well as the accompanying shrapnel effect of the projectiles hitting the masonry, signalled the end of masonry fortifications. The postwar fortifications program in 1870 involved building new earthwork batteries (which could absorb incoming artillery rounds), or placing earth on top of existing masonry forts, as was done at Fort Gorges.

In addition to the modifications at Fort Gorges, the Corps of Engineers quickly began construction of extensive earthen batteries at Fort Preble. The Corps also proposed an 1800 foot long earthwork battery of thirty-four guns for Portland Head directly behind the lighthouse, as well as a forty-gun battery on Little Diamond Island.

Title to the land at Portland Head was secured and construction began in 1873. Before work ceased uncompleted three years later, only six gun platforms and six storage magazines had been completed, along with extensive work on the earth embankment. Rapid advances in naval armament and armor-plated hulls had also rendered ineffective these projected defenses designed for heavy guns with a range of three to four miles.

CAPE ELIZABETH, 1890s

Cape Elizabeth encountered the beginnings of a profound change in the town in the 1890s when the United States government established a military reservation at Portland Head in 1891, that expanded into a large coastal defense installation by the end of the decade. However, two other local events also had great impact on the town. In March 1895 the northern half of Cape Elizabeth separated and became the town of South Portland (incorporated as a city in 1898), leaving the southern, rural, seacoast half as Cape Elizabeth. In June 1898 the local trolley system opened Cape Cottage Park just north of the sprawling military installation then under construction.

As part of the Gay 90s phenomena that overwhelmed the country, every self-respecting trolley company built at least one trolley park at the end of the line beyond the single nickel fare in order to produce extra ridership and at double fare. These parks provided leisure activities in a landscaped park setting usually on lakes, rivers, or the seashore. By 1907 there were

Cape Cottage Casino with the Goddard Mansion beyond.

467 trolley parks in the country, which were the forerunners of the amusement parks of today.

The second of three parks ultimately built at the ends of the system serving Portland and vicinity (the other two at Riverton Park in Portland and Underwood Springs in Falmouth), Cape Cottage Park offered the ultimate in relaxation: shore dinners at the casino (restaurant, not gambling), concerts, the latest in nationally-known summer stock theatre productions, leisurely strolls among the gardens and along the shore, or sitting on the wide verandas. A dock provided access to a small Casco Bay steamboat. The park was a great attraction for both locals and tourists until World War I.

The availability of the automobile signalled the decline of the trolley park, and Cape Cottage Park struggled until its closure in 1923. The park was developed into houselots, and is not recognizable today except for the surviving casino, now a private home that was reduced from two stories to one.

Another event occurred in Cape Elizabeth in the 1890s that had no significance locally, but was to have a cultural impact nationally. John M. Feeney was born in a farmhouse a few miles from Portland Head. Moving to Portland as a child and graduating from high school there, Feeney joined an older brother in Hollywood, and changed his name to John Ford.

Ford (1894-1973) became what many believe was the greatest movie director of all time, directing more than 200 films (including several John Wayne classics) and winning six Academy Awards. He received the first Life Achievement Award from the American Film Institute, as well as the Presidential Medal of Freedom from President Richard Nixon.

MODERN DEFENSES AND PORTLAND HEAD, 1891-1898

The War Department's Endicott Board Report of 1886 recommended radically new defenses for the seacoast, but substantive work did not begin for a decade. Portland Harbor was listed tenth on the priority list in terms of strategic defense out of twenty-seven locations nationwide, following New York City, San Francisco, Boston, Great Lakes, Hampton Roads, New Orleans, Philadelphia, Washington, D. C., and Baltimore. However, the total expenditures proposed for Portland were only exceeded in four locations: San Francisco, New York City, Hampton Roads, and Boston. Clearly, Portland Harbor was recognized for its importance.

In addition to the economic importance of Maine (lumbering, shipbuilding, and fishing), Portland's deepwater harbor was the closest to Europe, and could provide a defended anchorage for an American fleet to counter an enemy fleet which might take over Halifax or St. John in the Canadian Maritimes as a base of operations against the American coastline.

In 1891 the Army began building a series of mining casemates to control electrical submarine mines to be laid in

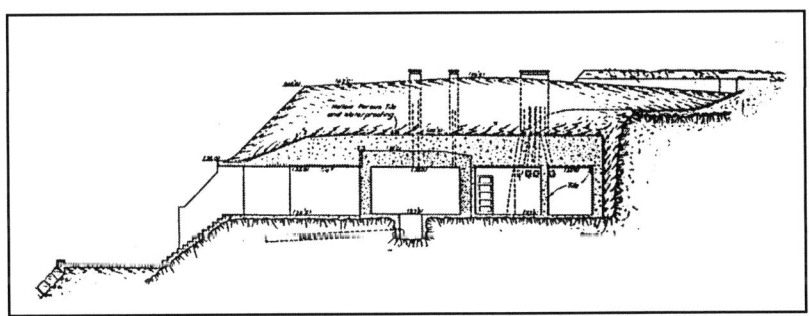

National Archives
Cross-section of the underground 1891 mining casemate at Ship

strategic channels in wartime. The buoyant mines would be strung together and positioned eight to forty feet below the water's surface, able to be fired electrically from the casemates. Three casemates were completed in Casco Bay, two on Great Diamond Island and one at Ship Cove on the military reservation at Portland Head.

The new network of defenses envisioned for Portland Harbor were to be located at existing Fort Preble, as well as Portland Head, Cushing Island, Great Diamond Island, and Cow Island. These new defenses involved large mortars and guns hidden behind massive concrete and earth berms, rather than cannon firing from within granite-walled fortresses.

The new defensive system located forts as far in front of the defended port as possible in order to engage any invading fleet beyond that fleet's range of the harbor. Between 1893 and 1909, twenty-five batteries emplacing seventy-three guns or mortars of 3-, 6-, 8-, 10-, or 12-inch caliber (referring to shell diameter) were constructed at these locations, providing overlapping fields of fire defending all entrances to Portland Harbor to a distance of about eight miles seaward. Except for the standard design mortar batteries of eight pieces, the design of a gun battery might provide for one to five guns depending on its tactical mission, although none in Portland Harbor had more than three.

Firing position: 10–inch gun in Battery Sullivan emplacement # 1

Recoil position being swabbed out: 12-inch gun in Battery Blair emplacement #1 (c1910).

Loading position: 12-inch gun in Battery Blair emplacement #1,

    The modern gun batteries were widely dispersed and hidden from view at sea. While the mortars were totally obscured, the other large guns (8-inch or above) were mounted on disappearing carriages, and hidden behind protective cover except for their brief firing sequence when the massive arms on the sides of the guns pivoted the guns into firing position. After the gun was fired, the recoil would return it to the protected loading position.

    The large gun batteries were protected on three sides by

A Seacoast Gun Battery

1. Exterior Slope of Parapet.
2. Superior Slope of Parapet.
3. Interior Slope of Parapet.
4. Blast Slope or Apron.
5. Magazine Ventilator.
6. Interior Crest.
7. Traverse.
8. Interior Wall.
9. Traverse Wall.
10. Canopy.
11. Reserve Table.
12. Delivery Table.
13. Observing Station (Crow's Nest).
14. Gun Platform.
15. Loading Platform.
16. Platform Stairs.
17. Corridor.
18. Corridor Wall.
19. Latrine.
20. Parade Wall.
21. Approach.
22. To Oil and Tool Room.
23. To Shell Room.
24. To Magazine.
25. Battery Parade.
26. Office.
27. Gallery.
28. Crane.
29. Interior Slope of Parados.
30. Traverse Slope of Parados.

Frontispiece.

thick concrete walls combined with earth cover, some to a thickness of sixty feet. Ammunition magazines and shell preparation tables were located at lower levels of the batteries, along with plotting and communications rooms, all accessible at the unprotected landward rear of the battery. Shells and powder were transported to the gun platforms by mechanical hoists.

While some of the 6-inch guns were mounted on disappearing carriages, others as well as most of the 3-inch guns were mounted on non-disappearing pedestal mounts, also called barbette mounts, loading and firing over lower-walled batteries. Since these latter guns were half exposed to enemy fire, they were designed with thick shields for limited protection of the guns and their crews. Some 3-inch guns were mounted on balanced pillar mounts, also called masking parapet, whereby the gun remained above the parapet for loading and firing but could be lowered for concealment.

Each gun battery was formally named for a deceased officer. A large enamel sign with white lettering on a blue background with the word battery and the last name of the honored officer was attached to each battery.

Primary armament (8-inch and above) was designed to penetrate the side, turret, and deck armor of heavily armored warships, and carry explosive charges into the interiors. The 12-inch mortars were specifically designed to fire at high angles of elevation so that shells would descend on the unarmored decks.

Intermediate armament (4.72- to 6-inch) was designed to attack lightly armored or unarmored vessels. It could also be used in a supplemental role with either primary or secondary armament.

Secondary armament (3-inch and below) was designed to defend mine fields, attack lightly armored or unarmored vessels, or defend against small boats and landing parties. Intermediate and secondary armament were designed as Rapid-

Left: Typical seacoast gun battery (1910).

William B. Jordan, Jr.

10-inch gun barrel being hauled to Portland Head from Fort Preble in August 1897.

Fire (called Quick-Firing by the British) in terms of loading and firing.

Only two of the gun batteries in Portland Harbor, both at Portland Head, were completed and turned over to the artillery in time for the Spanish-American War in 1898. Batteries Sullivan and DeHart, north of the entrance to the lighthouse, mounted three and two 10-inch Breechloading Rifles on disappearing carriage mounts, respectively, each capable of firing a 600 pound shell eight miles. These batteries were named for Major General John Sullivan (1740-1795) and Captain Henry V.

Portland Press Herald

Emplacement #3 of Battery DeHart (1973) before it was buried, with Portland Head Light beyond.

De Hart (1834-1862). The former was a New Hampshire officer and politician who had been a Maine resident in childhood, while the latter was a New Yorker killed in action.

After the outbreak of war in April 1898, a detachment of the Regular Army 2nd Artillery Regiment from Fort Preble was quickly moved to Portland Head. A searchlight to scan the water was placed on the bluff south of the lighthouse. The 2nd Artillery detachment was replaced the next month by elements of the Regular Army 7th Artillery Regiment sent up from New York City, as well as a supporting detachment from the 1st Connecticut Infantry Regiment, U. S. Volunteers, all of whom were housed in tents.

The reservation at Portland Head was formally established in May 1898 as a subpost of Fort Preble, but became an independent post in November. The big guns at the fort were in readiness throughout the short war, but were not even test fired until late August, two weeks after the end of the war. While there had been a great deal of apprehension that the concussion from the firings would damage the lighthouse, the fears proved groundless.

FORT WILLIAMS, 1899-1916

William B. Jordan, Jr.
Brevet Major General Seth Williams, U.S.A.

On 13 April 1899 the post at Portland Head was formally named Fort Williams in honor of a Maine native and West Point graduate, Brevet Major General Seth Williams (1822-1866), adjutant general of the Army of the Potomac 1861-64, and General Grant's inspector general 1864-66. Williams was a member of a politically prominent family of Augusta, Maine. His father Daniel (1795-1877) was elected to several state offices, and served as mayor and as county judge of probate, while his uncle Reuel Williams (1783-1862) was a U. S. Senator in 1837-43, and first cousin Joseph H. Williams (1814-1896) was governor in 1857-58.

Cape Elizabeth Historical Society
Post headquarters (1899-1911) with battle commander's observation station in the left rear.

Cape Elizabeth Historical Society
Stable, later salvage warehouse.

Cape Elizabeth Historical Society
Quartermaster storehouse #2 with stone crusher in the distance.

Several frame structures were built at the fort in 1899, some temporary but also including a standard design post headquarters, the first of the large officers' quarters on "Officers Row", and quartermaster buildings which were used to store non-ordnance type supplies, materials, and foodstuffs essential to the functioning of the fort, as well as to perform non-ordnance maintenance and repair. In 1900 the Army acquired additional land for Fort Williams which included the Goddard Mansion built by a prominent local businessman in 1858.

John Goddard (1811-1870) had hired a notable New York architect, Charles A. Alexander, to design the imposing stone mansion. Goddard briefly served as a colonel in a Maine cavalry

Cape Elizabeth Historical Society
Goddard Mansion, pre-Army.

Cape Elizabeth Historical Society

Goddard Mansion (c1940).

regiment in 1861, but resigned before the regiment left for war service. The acquisition of the mansion property extended the fort's northern boundary to Cape Cottage Park. A final piece of land was acquired in 1902 along the southern boundary.

Starting in 1901, large, neo-classical brick buildings of standard design were built for various non-tactical uses, such as: officers' quarters, non-commissioned officers' (NCO) quarters, enlisted barracks, hospital, gymnasium, post exchange, guardhouse, bakery, laundry, fire station, and quartermaster storage.

Officers Row.

Cape Elizabeth Historical Society

Non-commissioned officers' (NCO) quarters

Gymnasium

Barracks with hospital stewards' quarters at right.

Each structure at this and every military post was numbered to provide permanent and quick identification. Fort Williams had five barracks constructed between 1901 and 1910: a double barracks for one company of men on each end, three single company barracks, and a smaller band barracks for forty-eight band members.

Each company of artillerymen had an authorized strength of a little over 100 men. With five companies of artillerymen, Fort Williams was known as a five-company post. The old Goddard Mansion was converted to NCO quarters. Incidentally, that house served as the setting for a mystery novel, *Midnight at Mears*

Cape Elizabeth Historical Society
Band barracks.

Battery Blair from the lighthouse with the National Guard camp beyond (c1935), gun invisible in loading position.

House, by Harrison Holt, published in Portland in 1912. Except for the procurement of fresh foodstuffs on the local market, the forts were self-sustaining communities, providing work, training, recreation, and living quarters for the garrisons.

In addition to batteries DeHart and Sullivan, the armament at Fort Williams was increased by the addition of Battery Hobart (1900), one 6-inch Quick-Firing Armstrong Breechloading Rifle on a pedestal mount, and Battery Blair (1903), which mounted two 12-inch Breechloading Rifles on disappearing carriage mounts. These batteries were named for 1st Lieutenant Henry A. Hobart (1790-1813) and Major General Francis P. Blair Jr. (1821-1875). The former was a Maine native killed in action, while the latter was a prominent Missourian. The 12-inch guns could fire a 1070 pound shell eight miles, the 6-inch guns a 106 pound shell eight

Battery Blair with gun visible just after it has fired.

Portland Press Herald

Parade wall of Battery Blair with battery commander's station to the right and plotting room below.

miles. Made in England, the 6-inch Armstrong gun was the only foreign-made gun to be mounted in the harbor defenses.

Between 1900 and 1909, over two dozen one or two-story fire control stations (of brick or stucco-type construction) were built at the Portland Harbor forts, and at Peaks Island, to visually plot targets for the guns by triangulation, especially the primary armament and some of the intermediate guns. Several methods underwent experimentation, but it was 1908 before an effective system was in place.

A vertical position finding system was developed by the turn of the century, replacing the reliance on visual observations and a gunner's skill. A single station placed about 100 feet above sea level mounting a depression position finder would generate data based on a vertical triangle involving the instrument in the tower, that instrument's height above sea level, and the target ship.

In 1905 the Army adopted a new system that had been tested in Portland and two other harbors, a horizontal base line method.

In this case the triangle was horizontal, involving instruments in two separately located base-end stations and the target ship as the corners of the triangle.

Observers in base-end stations would call in azimuth calculations of a target location to a central plotting room, which would enable the plotting room personnel to project the target's course and speed. With knowledge of the velocity of the artillery shells, the plotters could then target the ship at a particular location.

A third system was developed using a single station with a self-contained, horizontal base, range finder. This system was used by field artillery as well as in seacoast defense, relying on prisms reflecting light through lenses. All three systems were used into World War II.

To assist the personnel in the fire control stations in their calculations, a Tide Station provided periodic readings of the height of the tide, and a Meteorological Station provided data on the density of the atmosphere as well as the velocity and direction of the wind.

In September 1903 the Portland Harbor forts participated in extensive training exercises. Even with reinforcements from the 1st Massachusetts Heavy Artillery Regiment and the 1st Maine Infantry Regiment, National Guard, Fort Williams was ultimately captured by the "enemy" force, which had secretly landed at

Joel W. Eastman

Battery Keyes with mine observation station on the top, and the CRF station (1921) to the right.

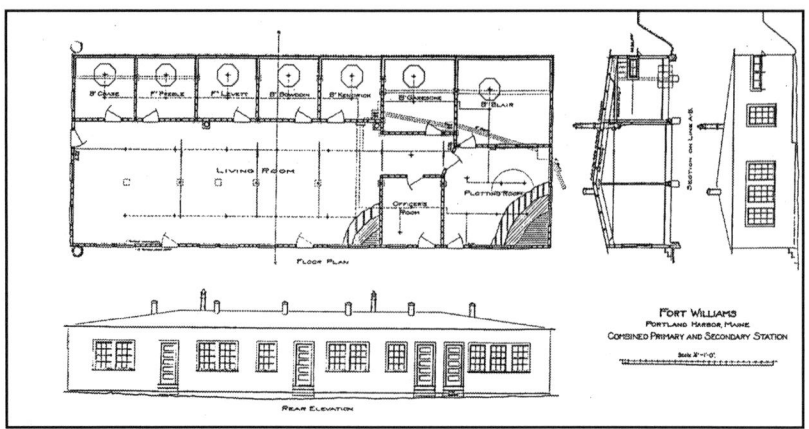

National Archives
1907 plan of combined observation station. Only two of the seven stations within were for guns at Fort Williams.

Crescent Beach and then made a surprise attack on the fort's undefended rear.

In 1906 the final two batteries at Fort Williams were completed: Battery Keyes, two 3-inch Rapid-Fire Guns on pedestal mounts, and Battery Garesche, two 6-inch Rapid-Fire Breechloading Rifles on disappearing carriages. The batteries were named for Major General Erasmus D. Keyes (1810-1895) of Maine, and Lieutenant Colonel Julius P. Garesché (1820-1862), a native of Cuba and a resident of Delaware who was killed in action.

Battery Keyes' two 3-inch guns could fire a fifteen pound shell four and a half miles, and were designed to defend against smaller, faster attack boats. The battery was supported by a searchlight located just to the north. The gun in Battery Hobart was removed in 1913, its responsibilities supplanted by Battery Keyes. Incidentally, the Camp Keyes complex in Augusta was also named for General Keyes. Receiving its name as a Civil War mustering camp, it has been the state National Guard headquarters since 1888.

Facing the open ocean, Fort Williams became the second largest of the harbor forts, and defended Portland Sound and Hussey Sound with six batteries of twelve guns spread over ninety acres. However, the smaller and long-established Fort Preble in South Portland remained as the headquarters of the Artillery

Mine wharf at Ship Cove.

District of Portland while the several forts were in various stages of construction during the first decade of the 20th century.

Seven fire control stations were built at Fort Williams in the period 1905 to 1908, which included base-end stations for gun batteries at other forts. One of four tide stations and one of three meteorological stations in the harbor were also built at the fort.

A group of structures was built around Ship Cove between 1907 and 1909 involved in the assembly, storage, and planting of mines, which, when strung in the channel, would be controlled by the nearby, newly-enlarged mining casemate. A mine loading room, service dynamite room, torpedo [mine] storehouse, cable tank, and a mine office were built. Also, a 50-foot by 140-foot mine wharf was built on the south side of Ship Cove, which was con-

Mining tramway from mine wharf with mining casemate in center, and Battery Hobart with lighthouse in distance.

Above: Army mine planting vessel in Portland Harbor (1941).
Below: Mines ready to plant (1941).

nected to the torpedo storehouse by a 2000-foot long, four-foot gauge mining tramway.

Two mine control stations to observe the minefields were built nearby, one south of Battery Hobart and the other atop Battery Keyes. This latter station still survives, and is a rare surviving example of stucco-type construction built in the period 1906-17 after the designs of Captain John S. Sewell. With large numbers

Left: Aerial photograph (1961) of Ship Cove looking east, showing mining facilities at the head of the cove.   *Portland Press Herald*

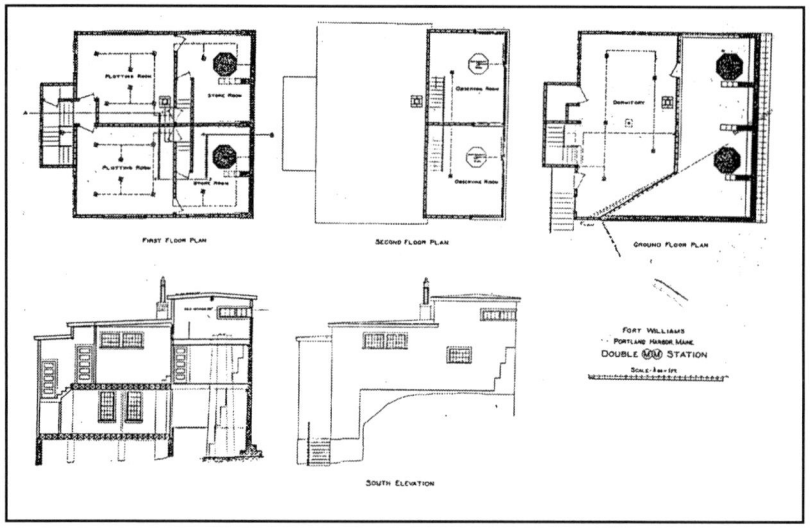

National Archives

1908 plan of double mine station located between batteries Hobart and Sullivan.

of new fire control structures awaiting construction because of the adoption of horizontal base-lines, the "Sewell-type" construction became financially attractive over the more substantial but far more costly brick used for earlier stations. Incidentally, the prototype Sewell structure tested had been a double mine station at Fort McKinley on Great Diamond Island.

By 1909 the tactical elements of Fort Williams at Portland Head were substantially complete, as were those at the new Fort Preble (a two-company post), Fort Levett on Cushing Island opposite Fort Williams (a one-company post), Fort McKinley on Great Diamond Island (a seven-company post), and Fort Lyon on Cow Island (a small subpost of Fort McKinley). These forts were among seventy-eight so-called Endicott-era seacoast forts built on the Atlantic, Gulf, and Pacific coasts by the end of the first decade of the 20th century.

Fort Preble contained four batteries with nineteen guns and mortars (sixteen 12-inch mortars, two 6-inch guns, and a 3-inch gun), Fort Levett had four batteries mounting ten guns (three 12-inch, two 10-inch, two 6-inch, and three 3-inch), Fort McKinley had nine batteries of twenty-six guns or mortars spread over 200 acres (eight 12-inch mortars, and two 12-inch, eight 8-inch, four 6-inch, and four 3-inch guns), and Fort Lyon had two batteries with six guns (three 6-inch and three 3-inch). Fort McKinley was the tenth largest fort in the country, and the largest north of the New York City defenses on Long Island Sound. It defended Hussey Sound and the inner passage between the islands and the mainland.

The twenty-five batteries mounting seventy-three guns and mortars in Portland Harbor represented about 6% of the total nationwide, among some 400 batteries mounting 1200 guns and mortars along the nation's coastline. The Army later reduced the number of mortars in each 12-inch mortar battery from eight to four to give crews more room, thus Fort Preble lost eight of their number and Fort McKinley lost four. In addition to the gun batteries and their fire control stations, forts Williams and McKinley each contained the aforementioned mining casemates as well as facilities to assemble and store the actual mines.

In 1907 the artillery branch of the Army had been split into the Field Artillery Corps and the Coast Artillery Corps, with the latter assigned to the various seacoast forts from Maine to Texas and on the West Coast. Regimental organization had been abandoned in 1901, replaced by separately numbered Coast Artillery companies. This system would be in place until shortly after World War I. The 5th, 9th, 49th, 89th, 107th, and 155th companies garrisoned Fort Williams at one time or another during that period.

Garrison life in the Coast Artillery was routine, involving training and readiness in a near caretaker status. Concerts by the Coast Artillery band were popular public events. In addition to the artillerymen, the fort garrison included detachments of Quartermaster and Medical Corps personnel to provide food, clothing, housing, and medical attention.

In January 1910 the 1st Maine Infantry Regiment, National Guard was redesignated as Coast Artillery, with the regimental organization dissolved into separately numbered companies,

Cape Elizabeth Historical Society
Commanding officer's quarters.

1st to 13th. Summer training was held at forts McKinley and Williams.

By 1911 the non-tactical support elements of Fort Williams were essentially complete. Additional officers' quarters, a guardhouse, and a fire station were among the structures built that

Cape Elizabeth Historical Society
Bachelor Officers' quarters (BOQ).

Cape Elizabeth Historical Society
Fire station.

year. The fire station was designed to house a fire engine, a hook and ladder, and two hose carts.

A large administration building was built on "Barracks Row" in 1911. Reflecting Fort Williams' size, key tactical position, and mainland location, the post acquired the headquarters of the harbor defenses from Fort Preble, and the new building was built

Barracks Row with Administration Building second from right.

to handle the increased responsibilities. The old post headquarters was sold to private interests and removed.

Throughout the years, additional structures, tactical and non-tactical, were built at the several forts for various needs. Among the major structures built at Fort Williams before World War II were an underground protected telephone switchboard and a disappearing searchlight in 1920, a newly developed Coincidence Range Finder (CRF) station for Battery Keyes in 1921, and several quartermaster garages and storehouses in the 1930s.

Land access to the fort was through five entrances on Shore Road, numbered one to five from north to south. Gate 1 provided direct access to most of the NCO quarters as well as the recreational facilities, Gate 2 provided direct access to the quartermaster buildings, vehicle garages, and the mining facilities, while Gate 3 was the more formal entrance at the center of the complex with Barracks Row on the left and Officers Row on the right. Gate 4 provided direct access to Officers Row, while Gate 5 provided direct access to the National Guard camp. In the early years, a tall picket fence approached both sides of Gate 3, where a sentry box was located, but fence, gate, and sentry box had all disappeared by the 1920s. For much of the time until World War II, the fort was wide open and accessible without challenge.

As the fort became physically complete, it moved closer to technological obsolescence similar to the short lives of

Main entrance, Gate 3, with sentry box on right and picket fence. (c1910).

Main entrance, Gate 3, in 1921 with no fence or sentry box.

defensive systems today. Within a decade all of the guns in the Army arsenal became relatively obsolete. Again, new advances in naval armament and gunnery, which gave ships longer range and higher trajectory angles, made the outranged batteries obsolete. In addition, the advent of aircraft further accentuated the potential vulnerability of the exposed batteries. The heyday of Fort Williams and the other forts of its type as the latest in the technological development of seacoast fortifications was in the period 1900-14.

FORT WILLIAMS, WORLD WAR I

After United States entry into World War I in April 1917, the Maine Coast Artillery companies were finally activated on 25 July and assigned to the Portland Harbor and Kennebec River defenses: headquarters and three companies to Fort Williams, two companies each to forts Preble and Levett, five to Fort McKinley, and one to Fort Baldwin at the mouth of the Kennebec River. This latter fort had been built in 1905-12 to protect the access to Bath Iron Works, and mounted three 6-inch and two 3-inch guns. The companies were quickly renumbered and reassigned in the harbor defenses in August, while two companies were sent to Massachusetts for guard duty at Camp Devens and at the Watertown Arsenal.

It was quickly seen that the German Navy posed no threat to the American seacoast, and several of the larger guns were dismantled at various forts and used to arm transport ships or to mount on railroad cars in Europe. Battery Garesche's two 6-inch guns were removed in 1917 and never replaced, while Battery Sullivan's three 10-inch guns were removed in 1918 and were not reinstalled until late 1919.

In December 1917 three Regular Army Coast Artillery companies at the Portland Harbor forts as well as nine of the thirteen Maine Coast Artillery companies were reorganized into the 54th Coast Artillery Regiment, with guardsmen composing four of the six companies of men. In late March the 54th Regiment sailed for Europe, arriving in France in early April, and eventually serving as railroad and tractor artillery until demobilization in 1919.

The four National Guard companies that had remained in Portland Harbor during the war were demobilized in January 1919, although large numbers of men had been transferred earlier to elements of the 26th Division, formed from New England National Guard units for service in Europe: in August 1917 to the 51st Field Artillery Brigade composing the 101st, 102nd, and 103rd Field Artillery regiments, and in January 1918 to the 101st Engineers. In May 1918 additional guardsmen from the Portland companies were reassigned to the 72nd Coast Artillery Regiment for service overseas.

In 1917 the Army quickly began a program to emplace two 3-inch Antiaircraft Guns at most forts. However, the guns were in short supply, and the program wasn't completed until 1921. Two of the guns were mounted on the earth berm of Battery Garesche at Fort Williams in 1920. Firing a fifteen pound shell, these guns had a vertical range of almost five miles, and a horizontal range of over seven miles.

The Army also initiated plans in 1917 to construct 12-inch long range batteries at ten harbors in the United States to deal with the threat of newer naval weapons. With a range of

Right: Fort Williams aerial photograph (1961) looking northeast. Former National Guard camp in the center. *Portland Press Herald*

National Guard camp with officers' tents in the foreground, enlisted mess halls beyond, and enlisted tents and Portland Head Light in the distance.

seventeen miles, a battery containing two of these guns was completed in 1920 at Fort Levett, Battery Foote.

FORT WILLIAMS, BETWEEN THE WARS

After the war, the Casco Bay forts were again manned by various Regular Army Coast Artillery companies. Recruitment of southern Maine residents into Coast Artillery companies for the state National Guard resumed in 1920. Three companies received federal designation that year, and three the following

National Guard camp with enlisted mess halls in the foreground and enlisted tents beyond. Note the small arms target pit in the left rear and the antiaircraft gun on Battery Garesche in the center rear.

Cape Elizabeth Historical Society
National Guard camp, 240th Regiment headquarters.

year. A regimental organization was formed in 1922 as the First Coast Defense Command, Maine National Guard, but redesignated as the 240th Coast Artillery Regiment, Maine National Guard the following year, when the numbered companies were redesignated as lettered batteries A through H (not to be confused with named gun batteries).

By 1931 the regiment's organization was completed with the addition of antiaircraft and searchlight batteries. Ten batteries of guardsmen drilled in armories in eight communities from Sanford to Rockland. The Milk Street Armory in Portland even had a practice 10-inch Rifle with which to perform simulated observation, plotting, and fire control functions.

The regiment conducted annual summer encampments at Fort Williams the first two weeks in July to perfect their skills on the real guns, as well as in antiaircraft and searchlight operations. A formal National Guard camp with mess halls and concrete pads for tents was laid out behind Battery Garesche in 1930.

As mentioned, the Army located two additional tactical elements at Fort Williams in 1920, a disappearing searchlight which could be raised and lowered by counterweight and the underground protected telephone switchboard, as well as the

Joel W. Eastman

Disappearing searchlight in lowered position, with counterweight at the left.

CRF station adjacent to Battery Keyes the following year. This station was a self-contained, horizontal base, range finder.

The Army also instituted a short-lived experiment using observation balloons as instrument platforms to assist in plotting targets for the gun batteries. Balloon hangars and hydrogen gas generator houses were built in 1921 at forts Williams and McKinley, but the program was quickly abandoned for a variety of reasons: wind, weather, flammable gas, and budget constraints. The balloon hangar at Fort Williams was then used

Joel W. Eastman

Disappearing searchlight being raised.

for storage until torn down in 1941; the same type of strange looking structure at Fort Worden State Park in Washington State was the site of the fight scene between Richard Gere and Louis Gossett Jr. in the 1982 movie, *An Officer and a Gentleman.*

During World War I homing pigeons had been used successfully to carry messages. The U. S. Army Signal Corps established pigeon lofts at various forts, including Fort Williams, about 1920. Although pigeons were again used effectively in World War II and pigeon lofts were retained until 1957 at Signal Corps headquarters at Fort Monmouth, New Jersey, the loft at Fort Williams was apparently gone before 1930, when the National Guard camp was built on the site.

In 1924 the Army reorganized the various Regular Army Coast Artillery companies into regiments, each with eight companies designated as a headquarters battery and seven batteries lettered A through G. The 8th Coast Artillery Regiment was organized at Fort Preble, the 9th at Boston Harbor, the 10th at Narragansett Bay, and so forth. While the Headquarters Battery of the 8th Regiment was stationed at Fort Preble, Battery E was detached for service in the harbor defenses of Portsmouth, New Hampshire, and the other six batteries were designated inactive. At this time, forts Williams, Levett, McKinley, and Lyon were designated as inactive caretaker Coast Artillery posts, although Fort Williams

Joel W. Eastman
Disappearing searchlight in raised position

Cape Elizabeth Historical Society
Balloon hangar with the central powerhouse at the right.

Above: The arrival in Portland Harbor of the 5th Infantry from occupation duty in Germany in March of 1922 aboard the USAT *Cantigny*.

Left: Fort Williams aerial photograph (1958) looking northeast showing the counterweight of the disappearing searchlight in the lower right corner.   *Portland Press Herald*

continued to host the annual summer encampments of the 240th Regiment each July.

Forts Williams and Mc-Kinley became active infantry posts with the arrival of the famous 5th Infantry Regiment in Portland from Europe aboard the USAT *Cantigny* on 21 March 1922. Distributed among forts McKinley, Preble, and Williams, the regiment established its headquarters at Fort Williams. In January 1923 the regiment became one of the first infantry regiments in the Army to replace mule-drawn wagons with motorized vehicles: forty-five trucks, cars, and motorcycles. The machine gun companies continued to use mules until 1939.

Within the first two years of the regiment's arrival in Portland, about 50% of the regiment had been discharged, with New England recruits filling the vacancies (most of whom were Mainers). The Maine contingent got so large that the *Maine Stein Song* was adopted as the official regimental marching song.

The regiment's main activity was training, but its sports teams were renowned for their prowess as they consistently beat local amateur teams in baseball, football, and basketball. In intraservice competition, the regiment excelled in those sports as well as track, pistol, and rifle contests. Band concerts, military parades, and sporting contests were always popular public events. On 1 December 1924, 5th Infantry band participated

5th Infantry parade with commanding officer's quarters beyond in the center.

5th Infantry machine gun practice at the target pit, with the National Guard camp beyond.

in the first radio show broadcast from Portland. Detachments of quartermaster and medical personnel continued to provide their services to the garrisons.

From the mid 1920s through the summer of 1939, the 5th Infantry Regiment provided the cadre for the Citizens' Military Training Camp (CMTC) at Fort McKinley, a program designed to provide a month of military style training for young men deemed potential officers. After the departure of the 5th Infantry in 1939, the CMTC continued the infantry-style training until August 1940 under the direction of reserve officers and 8th Coast Artillery NCOs.

Meanwhile, the seacoast defense picture at the forts was changing, reflecting the sober fact that most of the guns mounted in the period 1898-1909 were outmoded in terms of their

Formation marching through the National Guard camp with the two-story artillery engineer storehouse at the left.

Cape Elizabeth Historical Society
Officers' tennis court with militia storehouse on the left rear and twin radio towers in the background.

limited range. Technology had far surpassed the co-ordinated defensive systems in place at the various harbor defenses on the American coastline. By the 1930s, practical application of the new technology was evident in the world's navies as well as continuing development of more sophisticated aircraft.

At Fort Williams, batteries Hobart and Garesche were officially deactivated in 1929, reflecting the fact that the guns

Cape Elizabeth Historical Society
Gasoline storage tank and pump, which still survives, with veterinary office and artillery engineer storehouse beyond.

Joel W. Eastman
Surf breaking over the mine wharf at Ship Cove.

had been removed years earlier, while Battery Sullivan was decommissioned and Battery DeHart was placed in reserve on reduced maintenance by 1934. The Harbor Defense Command Post (HDCP) was located in the magazines and galleries of emplacements two and three of Battery Sullivan. In addition to a fort radio station, the Harbor Defense Radio Station as well as the Signal Station were established at Fort Williams.

After 1929 the mine wharf at Fort Williams was abandoned because it could not be used in rough weather. In addition, the wharf and the long tramway took a heavy pounding from the surf. Mines were still prepared at the fort, and hauled by truck to the wharf at Fort Preble, from which the mine planters were dispatched.

Two major fires broke out at Fort Williams eight years apart. On 5 August 1929 the roof of the double barracks was destroyed by fire, but was replaced by mid November. On 30 April 1937 fire completely destroyed the hospital annex along with most of the records of the medical detachment. The annex was located to the rear of the hospital, and contained the outpatient clinic and the pharmacy squad rooms.

In 1934 an additional 3-inch antiaircraft emplacement was constructed to the rear of Battery Garesche. However, the antiaircraft guns at Fort Williams were deactivated by 1938 although the fort retained the harbor command post for that

Cape Elizabeth Historical Society
Aftermath of 1929 fire in the double barracks.

activity, located in emplacement one of Battery Sullivan. The command post would also co-ordinate the eleven antiaircraft observation posts from Mount Agamenticus in York to Bald Head on Cape Small at the north end of Casco Bay. Although the 3-inch guns were deactivated, two platoons of four 50-caliber machine guns each were to be assigned to Fort Williams.

In addition to the permanent, fixed batteries (that were generally outmoded), Fort Williams' and Fort Preble's arsenals also included eight 155-mm. GPF Rifles, the standard heavy mobile artillery weapon. Towed to a location by tractor or truck and then stabilized for firing, this weapon fired a ninety-five pound shell ten miles. A gun shed was built at Fort Williams in

Cape Elizabeth Historical Society
Aftermath of 1937 fire which destroyed the hospital annex, with Battery Keyes and the searchlight shelter in the background.

Joel W. Eastman
155-mm. GPF Rifle being towed back to the gun shed next to the National Guard camp.

1934 to house two of those weapons; this structure is one of the few buildings to survive in adaptive reuse.

From 1933 to 1942 Fort Williams was the state district headquarters and induction center for the Civilian Conservation Corps (CCC), where 5th Infantry personnel provided two

Joel W. Eastman
155 mm. Rifle in firing position between Battery Blair and Portland Head Light during a summer camp (c1934) of the 240th Regi-

Cape Elizabeth Historical Society
CCC barracks with Portland Head Light beyond.

weeks conditioning for enrollees prior to their assignment to various WPA conservation projects around the state. The fort's Quartermaster Detachment was responsible for the construction of the twenty-eight camps statewide, and, with the Medical Detachment, responsible for the administration, safety, sanitation, and medical care for each. A cantonment of four barracks, two mess halls, and a recreation hall was erected in front of Battery Blair between Portland Head Light and Battery Garesche.

In the midst of the Great Depression and its massive unemployment, the CCC program provided work for young men between the ages of eighteen and twenty-five primarily on conservation projects. The enrollees at each camp were organized into one company of up to 200 men, commanded initially by Regular Army officers, who were soon replaced by reserve officers. Members of the Maine Forest Service, the U.S. Forest Service, the U. S. Biological Survey, and the U. S. National Park Service provided supervision and technical assistance for the enrollees in performing the various assignments.

Two of the twenty-eight camps were established at Fort Williams. The 165th Company served from May 1933 to June 1942 as a supply and administrative unit for the Maine district, the only camp to serve during the entire life of the program in the state. Its major responsibilities were procuring and shipping construction supplies to the other camps around the state, and keeping most records for the program.

The second Fort Williams camp, the 1131st Company, served from 1935 to 1939 doing construction work for the Army at the various Portland Harbor forts, including several projects at Fort Williams: tennis courts, bleachers, bandstand, swimming pool, showers, rock walls, and a lily pad pond.

FORT WILLIAMS AND PORTLAND HARBOR, 1939-1941

With the situation in Europe rapidly deteriorating, the 8th Coast Artillery Regiment was increased in strength between July and November 1939 through recall of scattered personnel. After the outbreak of war in Europe on 3 September, the 5th Infantry Regiment departed Portland Harbor for service in the Panama Canal Zone.

The reality of war became apparent to Portlanders on 12 September. A British freighter, the *Blairlogie,* had loaded scrap metal in Portland on 20-25 August before making its slow journey across the Atlantic, where it was torpedoed and sunk

Cape Elizabeth Historical Society
Lily pad pond built by the CCC, with band barracks beyond.

New theater built in 1938.

by a German U-boat off the Irish coast on the 11th, though all hands were saved.

In early November Colonel Robert C. Garrett was sent to Fort Williams with a contingent from Fort H. G. Wright, New York to organize a reactivated 68th Coast Artillery Regiment (Antiaircraft) (Mobile). Two battalions were activated, the First at Fort Williams and the Second at Fort McKinley. By the end of the year the regiment had reached 940 of its authorized strength of 1700 through transfers and recruitment. Rigid train-

Post exchange.

ing sessions were instituted to achieve a well-organized unit. On 15 May 1940 Battery A staged its first drill with a platoon of searchlights.

Another battery of the 8th Regiment was activated at Fort Preble in late July, and a week later, 5 August, the 68th Regiment was convoyed to its new duty station at Camp Edwards, Massachusetts, where it remained until ordered to the Boston Harbor defenses the day after Pearl Harbor. That regiment eventually landed in North Africa, Sicily, and Italy in 1942-43.

Most of the CCC cantonment between the lighthouse and Battery Garesche was torn down in May 1940, and seven large vehicle garages were constructed on the site, although three of those were dismantled two years later and reassembled elsewhere.

To supplement the 8th Regiment after the departure of the 68th, the various batteries of the 240th Coast Artillery Regiment, Maine National Guard were federalized at their home armories on 16 September (as part of the national federalization order) reporting to the various Portland Harbor forts the following week: the First Battalion assigned to Fort Williams

Portland Press Herald
Men of the 240th Regiment's searchlight battery loading onto trucks in the National Guard camp to join the searchlight battery of the 68th Regiment on field maneuvers in July 1940.

Cape Elizabeth Historical Society
Mess hall (1941) with barracks to the right, and the rear of the Goddard Mansion on the hill.

(less Battery A to Fort Levett), the Second Battalion to Fort McKinley, and the Third Battalion to Fort Williams (less Battery G to Fort Preble and Battery H to Fort McKinley). Regimental headquarters was established at Fort McKinley.

Within a week of reporting to Fort Williams, the Searchlight Battery (renamed Battery K in December) was called to action. The men of that unit were hastily called to the Portland Airport on 28 September to assist in landing Navy Blimp *TC13*, which was on its return home to Lakehurst, New Jersey after calibrating radio direction finders at the various Navy radio stations along the New England coast. After leaving Winter Harbor, the rigid-type blimp had encountered stiff winds causing extra fuel consumption, necessitating a precautionary stop in Portland for refueling. The craft circled the airport in windy conditions until the next morning, when the makeshift ground crew of the Searchlight Battery, under the direction of Navy officers flown up from Lakehurst, succeeded in landing the craft.

An aggressive enlistment campaign was initiated for the 8th and 240th regi-

Joel W. Eastman
Bell tower next to the chapel.

Cape Elizabeth Historical Society

Chapel (1941).

Janet S. Hill / Cape Elizabeth Historical Society

Interior of the chapel.

Cape Elizabeth Historical Society
Nurses' quarters / mess (1941), with one of the radio towers

ments in order to increase the regiments to their full authorized strength. In December newly-promoted Brigadier General Garrett was reassigned back to Fort Williams to command the newly-designated Harbor Defenses of Portland, which were quickly being brought to a wartime footing.

Schools were set up to give the new recruits basic training as well as Coast Artillery training. In February 1941 the remaining batteries of the 8th Regiment were activated, two each at forts Preble and McKinley. New temporary housing and other structures were built at the various harbor forts. Two barracks, two offices, a mess hall, and a recreation hall were built at Fort Williams in 1941 on the point of land between the Goddard Mansion and Battery Keyes, while several other structures such as nurses' quarters, officers' quarters, and a chapel were scattered about the fort.

The Army requisitioned one of the large Casco Bay Lines steamboats in 1941, the *Aucocisco* (which the Navy renamed the USS *Green Island* in 1942), to carry military personnel between the mainland and the harbor installations. The Navy also leased the island steamer *North Haven* from the Rockland-Vinalhaven Steamboat Company to ferry naval personnel.

With the federalization of the 240th Regiment and the

quick enlistment of hundreds of new recruits, the service detachments were increased and reorganized into the ll04th Corps Area Service Unit with headquarters at Fort Williams: quartermaster, medical, and veterinarian detachments, as well as Army nurses. A WAC (Women's Army Corps) detachment served in the harbor defenses through January 1946. The Quartermaster Detachment was charged with the supply, housing, transportation, and subsistence of the troops of the Portland Harbor defenses (and Portsmouth Harbor defenses until some time after they were separated in October 1940). The 50-bed hospital at Fort Williams was equipped for all types of medical treatment except obstetrics.

In 1941 Fort Williams was surrounded by a tall chain-link fence topped by barbed wire. Gates 2 and 3 were provided with sentry boxes, while the other three gates could be opened when warranted.

Although not in wartime intensity, the garrisons of the various harbor defenses were in a constant state of training, inspections, practicing, and alerts in order to maintain and refine a state of readiness. By the summer of 1941 the ten batteries of the 240th Regiment had been repositioned, with the First Battalion (A-B-C) at Fort Levett, the Second Battalion (D-E) at Fort McKinley and (F) manning the 155-mm. GPF Rifles at

Cape Elizabeth Historical Society
Hospital

Cape Elizabeth Historical Society
Gate 2 (c1935) with sentry box and no fence. Balloon hangar is on the right, with the quartermaster garage on the left and the torpedo storehouse in the distance.

Fort Williams, and the Third Battalion (G) at Fort Levett and (H-I-K) at Fort Williams, the latter three manning Battery Keyes, Battery Blair, and the antiaircraft searchlights, respectively. In the fall the latter two batteries of men were designated as alert security mobile units in addition to their harbor defense assignments. While batteries A, B, D, and I manned the various 12-inch gun batteries at three forts, everyone realized that these batteries were outranged by modern warships, were susceptible to aerial bombardment, and could not target and fire on small, fast attack boats.

In August 240th regimental headquarters was moved from

Cape Elizabeth Historical Society
Chain-link fence being erected at Gate 2 in 1941.

Cape Elizabeth Historical Society

New chain-link fence, sentry box, and salute gun at gate 3.

240th Regiment's Battery K (searchlight) in bivouac formation in front of their barracks (1941).

Camp of Battery K field maneuvers in Gorham (1941).

from Fort McKinley to Fort Williams. On 10-11 September 1941 the officers of the 8th and 240th regiments participated in an exercise designed to test their responses to various situations. No troops took the field during this exercise, as umpires headed by the commanding general of the Sandy Hook defenses graded the headquarter's exercise.

The exercise extended from Eastport, Maine to Long Island Sound, New York as elements of a fictitious enemy based in New Brunswick attacked by air, sea, and land. The officers of the Portland Harbor defenses had to contend with various scenarios throughout the day and a half exercise, never knowing where the full thrust of the invasion would be.

The *Portland Press Herald* captioned a first page article "Local Harbor Defenses Reel Under Attack in Exercises", as the fictitious events that unfolded included the bombing of Portland, destruction of its water supply, and infiltration of fifth columnists. Fort Williams was subjected to heavy aerial bombardment, and, before "considerable" casualties had been cared for, was peppered with gas, although the actual target of

Battery K vehicles.

the mock invasion turned out to be in Massachusetts.

Portland Harbor had been an important port since colonial times, and was the ocean terminus of a railroad connection from Montreal, Quebec since the 1850s. Portland had served as Montreal's winter port (while the St. Lawrence River was frozen) until the mid 1920s, when Canadian nationalism promoted the resurgence of Halifax, Nova Scotia as a port of entry.

However, in May 1941 an agreement was reached to construct a 236-mile crude oil pipe line from Portland to Montreal. Construction started in July, and the pipe line was completed and functioning in November. Portland's importance had also increased in November 1940 with a government agreement to locate a shipyard between Cushing Point and Spring Point in South Portland to build British freighters (a modified version of the *Ocean* Class cargo ships) and Liberty ships, armed transport vessels used to resupply beleaguered England and, later, American troops overseas.

Eventually, two shipyards with thirteen building berths were built, and thirty of the British freighters and 244 Liberty ships were delivered between March 1942 and October 1945, 9% of the total produced nationwide. By late 1944 the proficiency of the yards had reached the point where ships were completed from keel to delivery in fifty-three days. The yards employed 30,000 workers at the peak of production, including

Joel W. Eastman

Two 155-mm. GPF rifles in firing position in front of emplacement #3 of Battery Sullivan during the early months of World War II, with Portland Head Light beyond. The recoil gun pits at the rear of the guns, necessary for high angle fire, are still identifiable. today.

30-caliber machine gun and crew (1941).

3700 women. Several civilian housing projects were erected to house these wartime workers, including two large complexes that are still in use today: Redbank in South Portland and Sagamore Village in Portland.

One of the last two surviving Liberty ships in running condition of 2710 built at seventeen shipyards (and the only one remaining in original configuration), the SS *Jeremiah O'Brien* was launched in South Portland on 19 June 1943. Now a museum in San Francisco (the National Liberty Ship Memorial), the ship sailed to France in 1994 and recreated its participation in the Normandy invasion fifty years earlier (stopping in Portland on its return trip). Supposedly, it is the last survivor of the 5000-ship armada that participated in that invasion. Incidentally, the RMS *Titanic* engine room scenes in the 1997 movie *Titanic* were filmed on the *Jeremiah O'Brien* as it chugged back and forth on San Francisco Bay.

Fort Williams was also the site of a joint Army-Navy Harbor Entrance Control Post (HECP) established by the Navy in September 1941 to assist friendly ships in entering the harbor and to keep out the enemy. The post had a searchlight available for night observations, as well as an "Alert" firing battery available around the clock, Battery Keyes.

Battery F, 240th Regiment, air skirmish drill with gas masks

In late 1941 a U. S. Naval Station was established in Portland, with facilities ultimately spread out in Casco Bay. Portland quickly became one of the five largest centers of naval activity in the country, after Hampton Roads, San Diego, San Francisco, and Newport, reflecting Casco Bay's strategic position in the supply lanes of the North Atlantic, as well as the pipe line and the shipyards.

In addition to pier facilities and offices at a Section Base on the Portland waterfront, fleet anchorage areas were designated for ships of the North Atlantic fleet. Large underground storage tanks were constructed at a fuel annex on Long Island, which was also the site of a seaplane base and a recreation center. A naval barracks and a fleet training center were established at Fort McKinley on Great Diamond Island, while an outdoor recreation center and a firefighting school were created on Little Chebeague Island. In fact, Fort McKinley was primarily a Navy reservation by 1943.

On 31 October 1941 an Iceland-based destroyer, the USS *Reuben James,* became the first American ship lost in World War II while doing duty with the Convoy Escort Force. The home port of the ship was Portland, where the families of sixty crewmen lived. One of five destroyers protecting a convoy of supply ships bound for England from Halifax to a point west of Ireland where the British Navy would relieve the American warships, the *Reuben James* was torpedoed by a German U-boat, the *U-562,* five weeks before Pearl Harbor, with a loss of 100 of its 144-man crew. The ship became the subject of a popular

Battery F antiaircraft defense firing (1941).

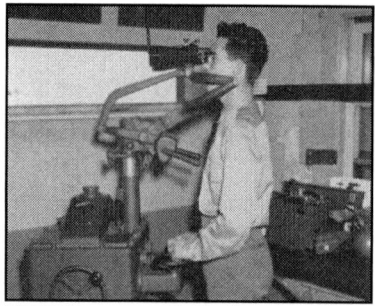 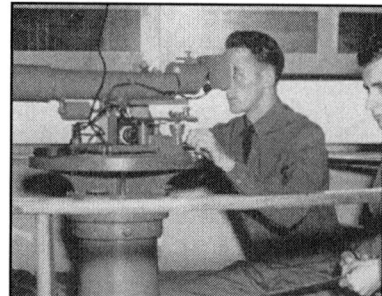

HECP searchlight control   **HECP observation instrument.**

World War II song written by folk-singer Woody Guthrie (father of Arlo) to memorialize the sinking.

In November 1941 naval command of all destroyers in the Atlantic was established in Portland Harbor. A large Navy vessel, the USS *Denebola,* served throughout the war as the command ship for the admiral commanding the Atlantic destroyers (COMDESLANTS).

In October 1941 Navy personnel had begun installation of submarine nets, booms, and gates in the various passages of Casco Bay. Although work was not completed on the main ship channel off Fort Williams until October 1943, work on the other five passages had been completed in May 1942. Whitehead Passage and Chandler Cove were permanently closed, and gates were installed at Hussey Sound, Littlejohn Passage, and Drinkwater Passage. Navy guardships were established at each location. Hussey Sound was restricted to naval vessels. The Navy also laid underwater cable loops to aid in submarine detection, while the Army laid fields of buoyant mines.

FORT WILLIAMS AND PORTLAND HARBOR, 1941-1943

After the declaration of war on 8 December, Fort Williams and the other harbor forts were brought to a wartime footing of readiness. Training and alerts were intensified. On the day of the declaration the big guns of Battery Blair were test fired at a target being towed offshore. A *Portland Press Herald* article headlined "Big Guns Make Garages Quiver" noted that the concussion from the firing of fourteen shells blew out the

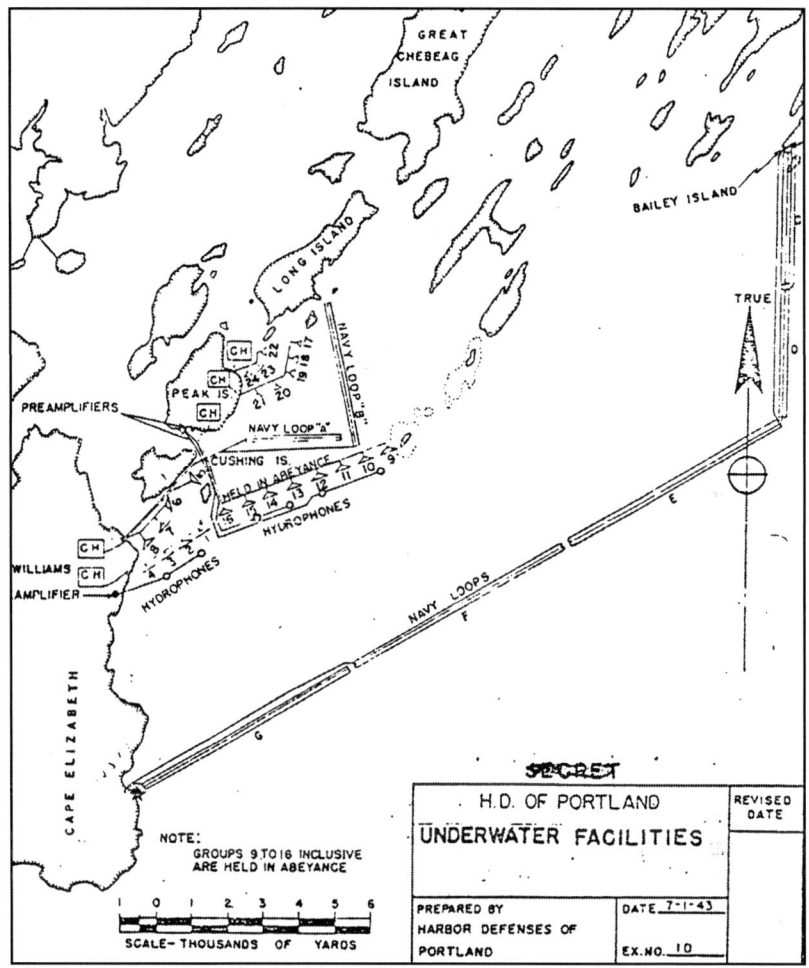
National Archives
Underwater defenses (1943).

ends of four large vehicle garages built a year and a half earlier in front of the battery.

In late December the Eastern Theatre of Operations was established, absorbing the Northeast Defense Command created the previous March. This theatre was renamed the Eastern Defense Command in March 1942, and co-ordinated defenses from Maine to Florida. The Northeast Frontier Defense Sector in Boston was the intermediate command over the New England

Portland Press Herald

Battery Blair 12-inch gun #2 in firing position (1926), with Portland Head Light beyond.

defenses. On 11 December 1941 the Portland Frontier Defense Sub-Sector (renamed the Portland Subsector the next month) was established with headquarters at Fort Williams. Under the command of Brigadier General Harold F. Loomis, this subsector exercised control of the Harbor Defenses of both Portland and Portsmouth. Manned by the 22nd Coast Artillery Regiment, the Portsmouth Local Sector included Camp Langdon and forts Constitution and Stark, all in New Castle, New Hampshire, as well as Fort Foster in Kittery, Maine. The number of Army personnel serving in the Portland Subsector (Portland and Portsmouth defenses) on 11 December stood at 3849; by the end of January the strength had increased to over 4900.

On 11 December Battery D of the 8th Regiment at Fort Preble was sent to former Fort Baldwin, located on a hill above the village of Popham Beach at the mouth of the Kennebec River, to protect access to Bath Iron Works with that regiment's four 155-mm. GPF Rifles. After World War I the post had been in an inactive caretaker status until the Army deemed it obsolete in 1923, and removed the guns and sold the installation to the state the following year. By June 1942 the mobile guns were emplaced on fixed Panama mounts, which allowed the guns to traverse in a 360° circle. Battery D remained there until June 1943, when it was relieved by another unit.

On 12 December Battery F of the 240th Regiment took the regiment's four GPF Rifles to Biddeford Pool to establish the southern limits of the harbor defenses. Fixed Panama mounts were subsequently built for these guns. Battery F remained there until February 1943 when it was relieved by Battery E of the 22nd Regiment from the Portsmouth defenses.

Along with the mobile 155-mm. GPF Rifles, the harbor defenses also acquired the more modern 3-inch Antiaircraft Guns on mobile mounts. Firing a 12.7 pound shell, the gun had a horizontal range of eight miles and a vertical range of five and a half miles. For traveling purposes, this gun mount would fold up more compactly than the 155-mm. GPF. From the traveling position, a well-trained gun crew could have the gun ready to fire in less than ten minutes.

In addition to the coast artillerymen and the support organizations, each subsector was assigned a combat team composed of detachments of infantry, field artillery, engineers, and service personnel. From 26 December 1941 until 30 November 1943, a combat team was assigned to the Portland Subsector, and headquartered at Saco, Maine, although elements were strung out along the coast from Damariscotta to Machias.

Cape Elizabeth Historical Society
Vehicle garages from the lighthouse property.

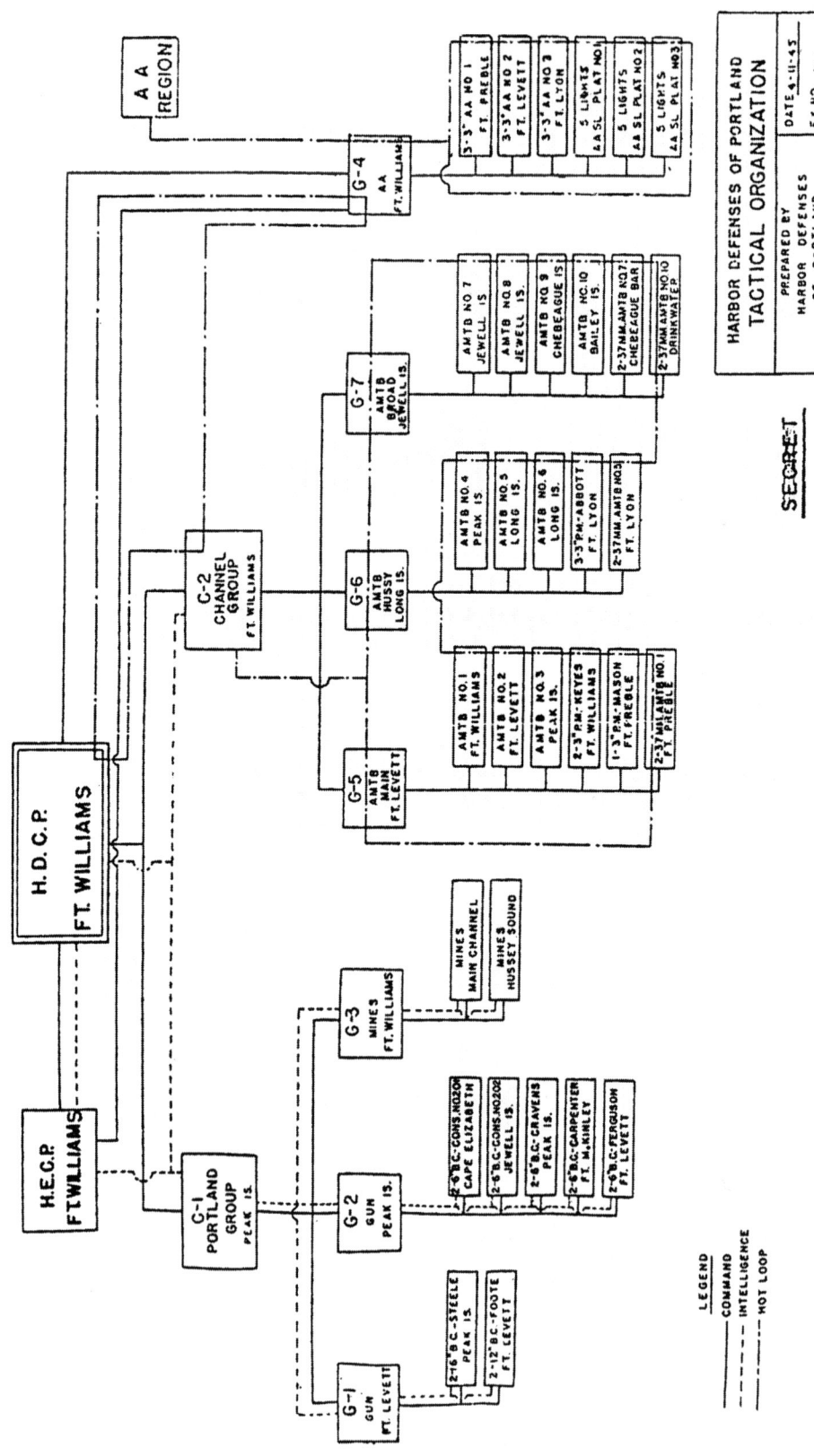

Portland Press Herald

Men of the 240th Regiment with a 3-inch mobile antiaircraft gun behind Battery DeHart, with Battery Blair to the right.

Located at the main entrance to Portland Harbor, Fort Williams played a key role in directing Army activities in Casco Bay, and in co-ordinating those activities with the Navy. In addition to housing the HECP, the fort maintained the headquarters of the Portland Subsector, the Harbor Defenses of Portland, the Harbor Defense Control Post (HDCP), and the 240th Regiment. Fort Williams was also the command post of one of the two subordinate command groups (C-2) under the HDCP, as well as for two of the seven subordinate gun groups in the harbor defenses. Gun Group 3 co-ordinated the two harbor mine commands: (1) controlling the main channel and (2) Hussey Sound. Gun Group 4 was the Antiaircraft Intelligence Command Post for the harbor. The only Meteorological Station was still at Fort Williams, while the only Tide Station was at Fort McKinley.

After United States entry into the war in December, Navy patrol boats and minesweepers became an active part of the harbor defenses. A humorous confrontation occurred in early 1942 between the HECP at Fort Williams and an arriving com-

Left: Harbor defense tactical organization chart showing Fort Williams' role . *National Archives*

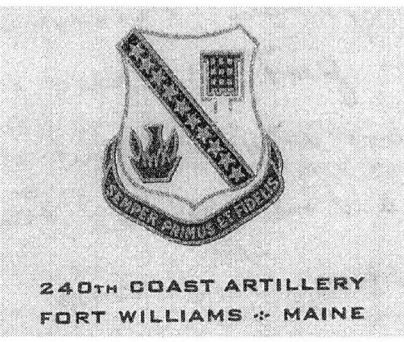

Two types of Fort Williams headquarters letterhead stationary during World War II.

mercial ship. The well-known collier *Oakey L. Alexander* had been making the coal hauling run between Norfolk, Virginia and Portland for over a decade. On one of its routine scheduled trips, the ship proceeded toward Portland Sound in the early daylight. A Navy HECP signalman flashed the challenge of the day, which was answered by an expired response. Repeated challenges were met by the same response. Orders to stop were ignored by the ship, including the threat to open fire. Ignoring the rules to open fire, the HECP officers decided on an ingenious alternative. The order was given to discharge the fort's blank-firing salute cannon with its ferocious muzzle flame several minutes before scheduled reveille. The ship quickly stopped and gave the appropriate response, and was allowed to proceed.

In a postscript five years later after the war, the ship met a sudden end five miles away on the rocks off what is now Two Lights State Park. On its 850th trip into Portland Harbor, the ship broke in two in a violent storm on 3 March 1947. The captain skillfully guided the aft portion and its watertight compartment onto the ledge near shore, and the entire crew was rescued with a breeches buoy by Coast Guardsmen from the nearby Life-Saving Station.

During the height of the war, Casco Bay was often filled with dozens of Navy ships from patrol boats to battleships for resupply, refueling, convoying, training, or crew liberty. In a sidelight, author Bob Reiss wrote a thrilling spy novel in 1983 set in wartime Casco Bay, *The Casco Deception,* about a Nazi attempt to take over one of the island forts in 1942 in order to turn the guns on the refueling supply convoys. It was an attempt to create panic on the homefront and force the American military to focus its attention on the American seacoast and defer European invasion plans for a year or two longer. The novel has no basis in fact, but could have been made more realistic if the author had done some basic research on the military presence in Casco Bay, as well as wartime materiel, procedures, and events.

On 5 June 1942 the light beacon in Portland Head Light at Fort Williams was discontinued, as were other lighthouses, as part of the Dimout Program. A great attempt was made to extinguish lights within three miles of the coast (later extended to fifteen miles). Civilian households were required to pull all shades down after 8:30 P. M. Maine was the closest point in the United States to Europe (German-held Norway in particular), and it was feared that the lights of coastal Maine could be used

Azimuth instrument in battery commander's station (1941).

Left: Pratt range board; center, deflection board; right, range percentage corrector (1941).

to assist German bombers on night raids to attack Portland, Boston, New York, or other targets. Failing to reach their assigned targets, the bombers could drop their bombs anywhere in Maine. Furthermore, the Navy felt that the lights of coastal Maine, particularly in urban areas, provided an illuminated backdrop for German submarines to locate and target any of the myriad of coastal freighters, convoys, or Navy vessels operating along the coast. In June Portland Airport became the base for Maine Civil Air Patrol (CAP) Group 111, one of two Maine units to assist the military on anti-submarine patrol.

Although German submarines operated off the coast in the Gulf of Maine during the entire war, the harbor defenses engaged in no hostile actions, other than occasional futile pursuit of reported German submarines by Navy ships. Only one submarine sighting occurred. On 22 June 1942 the magnetic loop closest to Cape Elizabeth registered a reading with no surface ships in the vicinity. Destroyers were dispatched, and an apparent sighting occurred off Bailey Island. Depth charges were made, and small oil slicks were reported the next day. However, discharging oil was a favorite trick used by submariners to fool those on pursuing surface ships into thinking that the depth charges had accomplished their goal. However, postwar research does not confirm any German U-boat in the area at that time.

On 1 July Brigadier General Thomas H. Jones succeeded General Loomis as commander of the Portland Subsector headquartered at Fort Williams. On the 6th of the month, Battery B of the 240th Regiment was relieved from Fort Levett, equipped with two 155-mm. GPF Rifles, and sent to Stockton Springs to protect the entrance to the Penobscot River for six weeks, before moving to Bailey Island to become the northeastern limits of the Portland Harbor defenses. In addition to the existing Portsmouth Local Sector, two other local sectors were established at Searsport [Rockland] and Ellsworth that month as subordinate elements of the Portland Subsector.

In July 1942 Colonel George E. Fogg (1878-1944), commanding officer of the 240th Regiment since its inception nineteen years earlier until the previous November, retired at the age of sixty-four with the rank of brigadier general. A Portland lawyer and a graduate of Bowdoin College, he had enlisted as a private in the Maine National Guard in 1909. Rapidly advancing in rank, Major Fogg served on active duty during World War I (1917-19) including a year in France and Germany with field artillery and infantry, before returning to the National Guard. He had thirty-three years service, with four years active duty in two wars. Fogg's unusual achievement in advancing from private to general exemplified the ideal and spirit of the citizen soldier in the National Guard.

One of the successors to General Fogg as colonel of the 240th Regiment, Alonzo B. Holmes (1896-1964) of Topsham had taken leave from Bowdoin College to take a short officer training course in 1918, and was commissioned a second lieutenant before returning to Bowdoin where he graduated in 1921. Joining the National Guard as a captain in the 240th Regiment in 1924, promoted to major in 1935, lieutenant colonel in 1940, and colonel in 1942, he was reassigned in 1943 to antiaircraft artillery serving overseas and became a brigadier general before war's end.

In order to meet the threat of advances in naval gunnery and heavily armored capital ships (battleships and cruisers),

Plotting board (1941).

as well as insure protection from carrier-based aircraft, the Army had begun planning the construction of new 6- and 16-inch gun batteries in July 1940, which could fire shells substantially farther than the pre-war batteries, fifteen and twenty-six miles respectively.

Land was acquired on Peaks Island in 1942, and construction began on a 16-inch two-gun battery, Battery Steele, under thick earth and concrete mounds. A concrete canopy projected over the openings for the gun barrels, from which shells weighing 2240 pounds would be fired. Battery Foote at Fort Levett was also provided similar protective cover. Land was also acquired for locations to emplace the new 6-inch guns on Peaks Island, Jewell Island, and a mile south of Two Lights in Cape Elizabeth. Curved steel shields entirely covered the exposed guns for these batteries.

In addition, seventeen new six-story fire control towers for the Portland Harbor defenses were built at various locations from Fort Baldwin near the mouth of the Kennebec River twenty-three miles north of Fort Williams to Cape Porpoise in Kennebunkport twenty-one miles south of the fort. Since the range of the newer weapons was beyond the horizon, these taller towers were necessary to overcome the visual limitations at ground level imposed by the curvature of the earth. Two of these towers at Fort Levett on Cushing Island may be seen from Fort Williams, while another was built at Two Lights near the 6-inch battery under construction (now Two Lights State Park).

The abandoned west light-

Fire control board (1941).

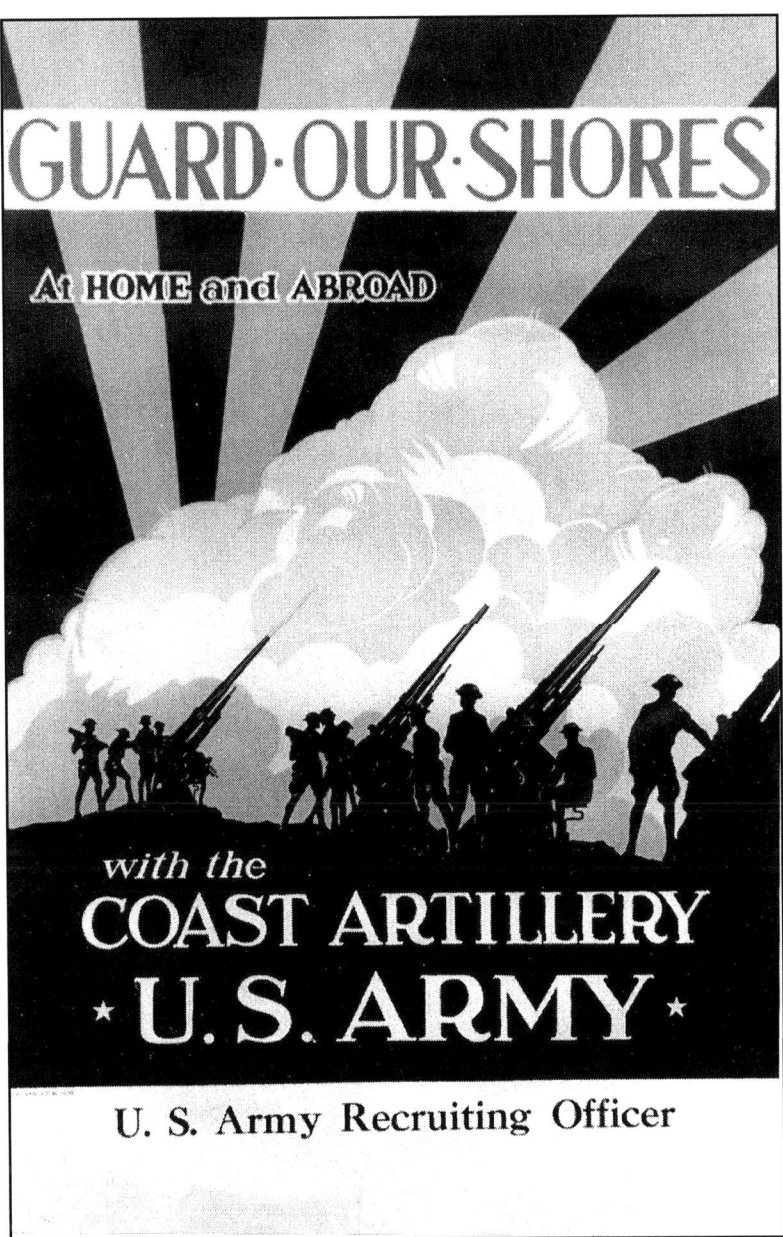

Roger W. Davis / Joel W. Eastman

World War II Coast Artillery recruiting poster.

house at Two Lights was also converted to a fire control tower. In a postscript, this tower was partially remodeled but never completed as a private residence some years after the war. Among its owners was the Hollywood actor Gary Merrill (1914-1990), who, having lived in Cape Elizabeth with his then-wife Bette Davis in the 1950s, returned years later after their divorce to make his home in the area.

In October 1942 Portland Harbor was the staging area for the large fleet of warships which was assembled to provide naval support for the Army's North Africa invasion. That same month construction began on Naval Air Station Brunswick (NASB), near the northern end of Casco Bay. Aircraft began anti-submarine patrols in January 1943, three months before the base was officially commissioned. In June the base began its major mission as a training center for British Royal Navy aviators.

Army strength in the Portland Subsector reached 6000 in October 1942, and the high water mark of 7295 in February 1943, which included both the Portland and Portsmouth defenses.

During the early months of 1943, the Army laid magnetic ground mines in the various channels to replace the electrical mines. The Army also built ten Anti-Motor Torpedo Boat batteries (AMTB) from Fort Williams to Bailey Island on the north end of Casco Bay to guard against fast-moving torpedo boats. The secondary mission of these batteries was antiaircraft defense. Initially, three batteries of two old 3-inch Rapid-Fire Guns were built on Peaks, Long, and Chebeague islands, but those guns were shortly removed and replaced when the other AMTB batteries were built, which also included forts Preble, Levett, and Lyon, as well as Jewell Island and Drinkwater Point in Yarmouth.

When finalized, each AMTB battery consisted of four 90-mm. guns (two fixed position and two mobile) and two 37-mm. guns (mobile), with 30-caliber machine gun support. Built between February and November 1943, AMTB #1, aka Battery 961, (minus the 37-mm. section at Fort Preble) was located in front of Battery Blair at Fort Williams, and had a range of seven miles. In addition to the two permanent mounts, several support structures were built in a small complex between those two guns and Battery Blair: two underground storage magazines, two generator shelters, a battery commander's station, and two barracks, while the nearby water heater house was converted to officers' quarters.

In terms of tactical importance, AMTB #1 was third on the list of twenty-four elements because of its key location, behind the submarine mines and AMTB #4 on Peaks Island. This battery replaced Battery Keyes as the "Alert" battery.

In September an Army surveillance radar unit (SCR 582) began operations at Fort Williams, and continued until war's end. The largest of eight radar units in the harbor defenses, the Fort Williams station had an average arc of detection exceeding twenty-two miles. However, radar was in its infancy, and was not entirely reliable.

The Army also located two of Casco Bay's twenty-seven new and powerful searchlights at Fort Williams (#s 7 and 8). The 800,000,000 candlepower searchlights had an illumination range of 7000 yards, with dual roles of seacoast and antiaircraft illumination.

With the availability of the newer armament, the obsolete guns of the older batteries in the harbor were ordered to be scrapped in late 1943. The 155-mm. GPF Rifles were also ordered to be removed and disposed of at the same time. Of the twenty-five batteries completed at the various harbor forts between

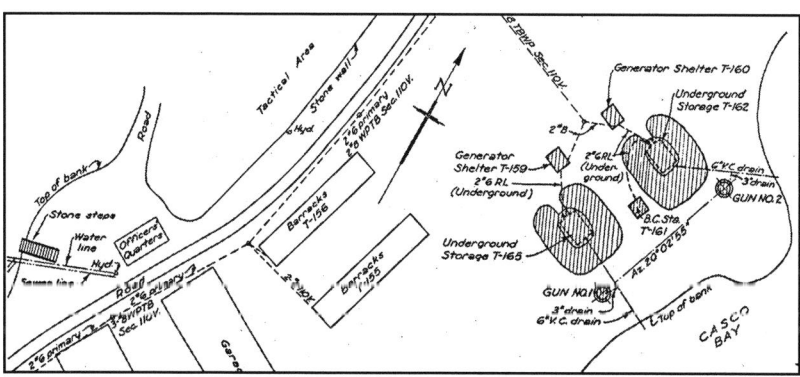

National Archives
Plan of AMTB #1, located south of Portland Head Light.

1898 and 1909, only five of the smaller ones were in service at war's end, the lowest elements on the tactical importance list. However, many of the guns were not scrapped until after the war's end.

By late 1943 the harbor defense armament included Battery Foote, three antiaircraft batteries, ten AMTB batteries, and five of the pre-World War I 3- or 6-inch batteries, as well as mobile 3-inch antiaircraft guns. Of the four original batteries still mounting nine guns at Fort Williams, only the two guns of Battery Keyes remained active thoughout World War II, although ranked twenty-third of twenty-four tactical elements in the harbor. Batteries Blair and DeHart were used for ammunition storage, while Battery Sullivan continued as the HDCP.

With the departure of Combat Team 81-2 at the end of November, a cavalry reconnaissance squadron was assigned to the Portland Subsector, with headquarters at Saco.

FORT WILLIAMS AND PORTLAND HARBOR, 1944-1945

Army coastal defense needs had substantially decreased by early 1944 since the potential of a threat by the surface German Navy had long evaporated. Fort Baldwin at the mouth of the Kennebec River was abandoned as a defensive position in February 1944, although a fire control tower was retained. The 6-inch Modernization Battery on Peaks Island, Battery Cravens, was completed and manned in early 1944, while the 6-inch battery on Jewell Island was relatively complete but remained in an unmanned, standby status. The battery at Two Lights never received its armament. Battery Steele (16-inch) was nearly complete later in the year, but remained in an unmanned, standby status, although it was proof-fired once. The battery was not fully completed until after the end of the war, only to be scrapped three years after that.

Downsizing and reorganization released many coast artillerymen for service with antiaircraft artillery (AAA) units in Europe or the Pacific. On 1 March the Portland Subsector was inactivated, and overall command of the Portland defenses once again reverted to the headquarters of the Harbor Defenses of Portland. General Jones was redesignated from commander of the subsector to that of the harbor defenses.

Except for Battery B to Fort Jackson, South Carolina, the 8th Coast Artillery Regiment was transferred from Portland Harbor in late March and early April to Camp Shelby, Mississippi and inactivated. The 240th Coast Artillery Regiment Band was transferred to Mississippi and redesignated in April, while the remainder of the regiment was redesignated in October while continuing to man the Portland Harbor defenses: the 185th Coast Artillery Battalion and the 186th Coast Artillery Battalion, each composed of a headquarters detachment and five batteries lettered A through E. However, the 185th and

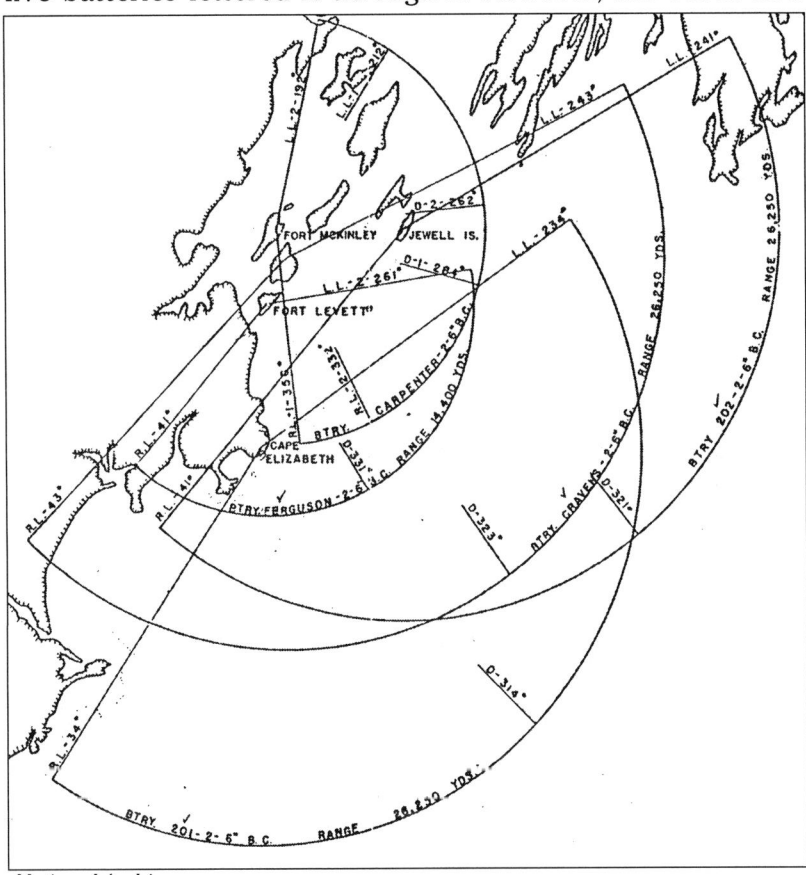

National Archives
Fields of fire of 6-inch batteries in 1945.

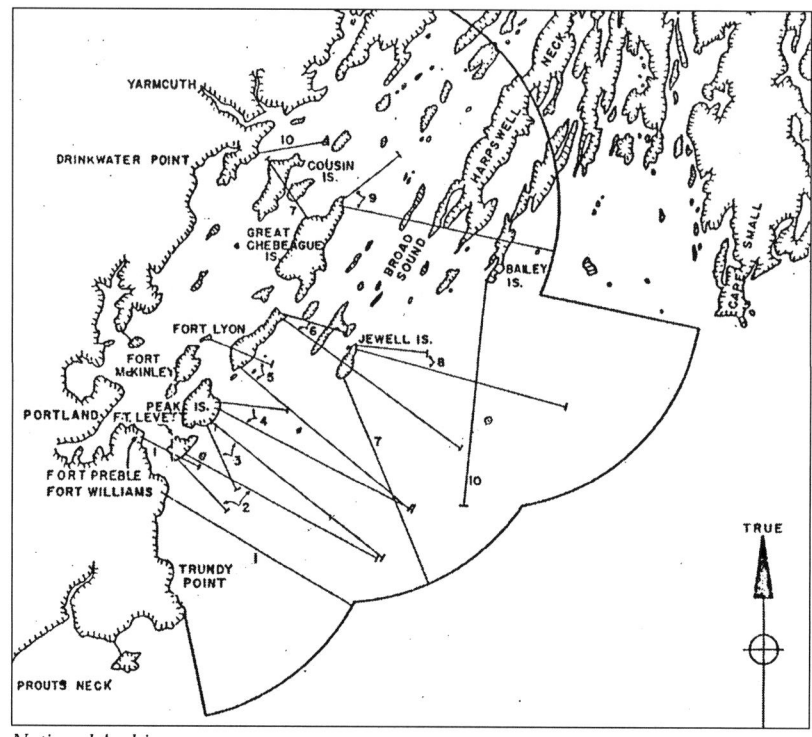

National Archives
Fields of fire of the AMTB batteries in 1945.

186th battalions were themselves reduced and redesignated as Harbor Defenses of Portland with a headquarters battery and six lettered batteries on 1 April 1945.

From January 1942 until May 1945, only twelve merchant ships were sunk off the New England coast by German U-boats, including two off Maine. Over 200 crewmen were lost, while twice as many were saved. Another U-boat supposedly shot down the sub-hunting U. S. Navy dirigible *K-14* on the night of 2 July 1944, which was operating about twenty-five miles south of Bar Harbor without its usual escort of a Portland-based destroyer. In addition, the *U-1230* dropped off two spies in Hancock, Maine in November 1944, who successfully made their way to New York City before being apprehended.

The most active period in terms of sea traffic in and out of Casco Bay was during the period of February to April 1944 preceding the Normandy invasion when there were forty to fifty warships based there in training. The most active single week was for the week ending 12 August when 530 vessels were allowed in through the gates of the main channel at Fort Williams (274) Hussey Sound (86), and Littlejohn Passage (170). A total of 558 vessels were let out during that period in nearly the same proportions.

At one time or another during the war, eleven of the Navy's battleships were in Casco Bay, including USS *Alabama, Arkansas, Indiana, Iowa, Massachusetts, Nevada, New Jersey, New York, North Carolina, South Dakota,* and *Texas.* However, those impressive vessels did not use the main channel at Fort Williams, instead using the deeper Hussey Sound.

In an officially unexplained disaster a little over two weeks before Germany's surrender, a Navy patrol boat, the USS *Eagle 56*, suddenly exploded, broke in half, and sank within sight of Fort Williams three miles offshore on 23 April 1945, killing forty-nine of sixty-two crew members. News of the disaster was not released until 9 May because of censorship restrictions. Postwar research in Germany credits the *U-853* with this sinking, but that U-boat itself was sunk less than two weeks later near Block Island, Rhode Island.

On 5 May 1945 German Grand Admiral Karl Doenitz ordered all submarines to surrender to the nearest allied port or ship. Of the five U-boats that surrendered to U. S. authorities, four were escorted to a designated rendezvous point off the Maine coast, from which they were taken to the Portsmouth Naval Base at Kittery, Maine.

From mid June until his death in late August, Vice Admiral Willis A. Lee, Jr., was in Casco Bay on special assignment as commander of a Composite Task Force (CTF 69) to develop anti-kamikaze procedures, but the war in the Pacific quickly ended after two atomic bombs were dropped in August.

With the conclusion of the war in Europe in May 1945, the Army and the Navy began the arduous task of drastically reducing the military presence in Casco Bay. Removing mines, nets, and booms that restricted sea traffic was a top priority. The beacon in Portland Head Light at Fort Williams was activated on the night of 28-29 June, after being out of service for three years.

The Army strength in the Portland Harbor Defenses was down to 1108 at the end of June, and 614 at the end of the year.

FORT WILLIAMS, 1946-1963

The various elements of the U. S. Naval Station Portland were inactivated by early 1946, as was the Naval Air Station Brunswick (although it was reactivated as Brunswick Naval Air Station in 1951). The various batteries of the Harbor Defenses of Portland were inactivated on 30 June 1946, and again redesignated to the same batteries of the 185th and 186th battalions in use before 1 April 1945. Army strength in Portland Harbor declined to 204 by the end of June, and was still at 197 at the end of March 1947, serving in caretaker status.

The war had made it quite clear that Coast Artillery forts were obsolete. The ease of successful amphibious landings in Europe, Africa, and the Pacific had shown that these forts were particularly vulnerable on their undefended landward rears if an enemy wanted to silence the guns in advance of a naval attack. Or an enemy could make an amphibious landing elsewhere, bypass the seacoast forts, and conduct a landward attack on their target city. While the airplane had posed a theoretical threat since World War I, the successive development of carrier-based aircraft, long-range bombers, the rocket by the Germans and the atomic bomb by the United States proved that the fixed defenses of seacoast forts were a thing of the past.

By 1948 most guns at all of the seacoast forts in the United States were scrapped. The scrapping of all the guns by 1950 was so complete that several types of guns do not survive anywhere.

The Coast Artillery Corps was officially abolished in 1950, replaced by the Antiaircraft Artillery Command. The Portland units were later redesignated as the 219th Antiaircraft Artillery Group, then the 240th Antiaircraft Artillery Group.

After the war Fort Williams retained the headquarters of the harbor defenses (such as they were), while Fort Preble became the headquarters of the Maine Military District, and the Organized Reserve Corps (ORC) in the state, commonly called Army Reserve, as well as its subordinate ORC School. On 7 August 1948 Regular Army personnel conducted a demonstration firing of the new recoilless 57-mm. and the 75-mm. Infantry Rifles at Fort Williams. However, of the Portland Harbor forts, only Fort Williams continued in an active status after the inactivation of the harbor defenses in June 1950. Fort Preble was transferred to the state and eventually became the campus of a vocational college, while forts Levett, McKinley, and Lyon were sold to private interests. The Modernization Program batteries on Peaks Island were also sold to private interests, while those on Jewell Island and at Two Lights became parts of state parks. Fort Baldwin at Popham Beach was also returned to the state for use as a state park.

As the only active Army post in Maine, Fort Williams became a recruiting, training, and administrative center for Army Reserve, National Guard, ROTC, and Civil Air Patrol activities

Cape Elizabeth Historical Society

Double mine station being burned by the Cape Elizabeth Fire Department, with a remnant of an 1873 magazine at the right.

in the state. During the Korean War, Maine draftees were processed through the fort. In March 1956 the Army renumbered all of the structures at Fort Williams, generating a completely different set of number designations.

After the closure of Fort Preble, Fort Williams received the former's designation as Headquarters, Maine Military District. In 1957 the fort was redesignated to Headquarters, U. S. Army Military District, Maine, which again was changed in January 1958 to Headquarters, Maine Sector, XIII United States Army Corps (Reserve). The 1128th ASU at Fort Williams (redesignated as 1128th SU in 1955) was responsible for reserve activities in Maine. Its subordinate unit, the 1033rd ORC School, Fort Preble, was activated at Fort Williams on 2 January 1951 with a fort name change. The school was redesignated the 1033d ARASU, USAR School, Fort Williams before 1955, when it became the 1033d ARSU, Fort Williams, USAR School. The school provided progressive training for Army reservists and development as instructors, while earning points for attendees for retention in the Active Reserve and for retirement..

Throughout the 1950s into the early 1960s, several other Army Reserve units were headquartered at the fort. Units based at Fort Williams included the 65th Ordnance Detachment, 173d Medical Battalion, 302d Military Police Battalion, 303d Army Postal Unit, 417th Infantry Regiment Headquarters, 752d Transportation Corps Company, 901st Field Artillery Battalion, 991st Signal Battalion, and the 1074th Transportation Corps Company. The medical unit was ordered to active service during the Berlin crisis in 1961.

In December 1958 the Maine National Guard received a new Adjutant General and commanding officer, Major General Edwin W. Heywood, a former resident of Portland. He had joined the 240th Coast Artillery Regiment in 1934 as a seventeen-year old drummer in the band, attended the annual summer camps at Fort Williams, and been promoted to 2nd lieutenant in 1939. When the unit was federalized in 1940, his battery was assigned to Fort Williams before moving on to Fort Levett.

Leaving the 240th Regiment in 1942 for ultimate service in the South Pacific, Heywood was discharged as a lieutenant colonel in the artillery in 1946. After the war he commanded the redesignated 240th Antiaircraft Artillery Group. He served as assistant adjutant general of the National Guard 1951-58, before reaching the top position. He served almost fifteen years as the state's top military officer under four governors until his retirement in 1973. His achievement was even more striking than General Fogg's as he went from drummer/private to major general.

By the early 1960s the Army re-evaluated its service needs, and decided to close Fort Williams. On 30 June 1962 the military presence at Portland Head ceased. On 30 July 1963 the Army declared the fort excess to military needs, and turned the post over to the General Services Administration (GSA) for disposition. The Headquarters, Maine Sector was re-established at the U. S. Naval Reserve Training Center in South Portland, and the 1033d ARSU on Westfield Street in Portland.

In August 1963 two episodes of the then-popular TV show *Route 66* were filmed in Maine, including a small part of one at Ship Cove at Fort Williams. In addition to series stars Martin Milner and Glenn Corbett, William Shatner of later *Star Trek* fame was the guest star in that episode.

FORT WILLIAMS PARK

With the exception of the lighthouse reservation, the GSA sold Fort Williams to the town of Cape Elizabeth on 1 December 1964 for $200,000. The town formed several successive committees, and initiated various studies to determine uses for the property starting in 1964. The Fort Williams Planning Committee, Urban Renewal Authority, Citizens Advisory Committee, Fort Williams Improvement Committee, and Fort Williams Study Committee all were formed within the first dozen years after the acquisition of the fort. In 1976 the Fort Williams Advisory Committee (later renamed Commission) was formed, and it is still in existence.

Unfortunately, nothing materialized out of the numerous proposals in the early years, and years of neglect and rampant vandalism reduced the once magnificent brick buildings to shambles. Most of the buildings were demolished and some of the batteries were filled in because of safety concerns starting in 1974. A handful of buildings were rehabilitated and occupied, and the town continues to use the underground mining casemate for civil defense purposes. While only a few buildings remain in adaptive reuse, over three dozen structures or batteries survive in large part. Nearly twenty more elements are easily identifiable by remains or foundations. And, numerous walkways, stairways, stone walls, fire hydrants, manhole covers, and sewer discharge pipes (at the base of the bluffs) from the Army period dot the landscape.

Foregoing the temptation to subdivide and sell this prime piece of real estate for generation of tax revenue, the town eventually decided to maintain the former fort grounds as an open space park available to all at no admission charge. In 1985 the Union Mutual Insurance Company (now UNUM) funded engraved interpretive signs scattered about the fort grounds depicting various military elements, based on excellent pen and ink drawings by Portland graphic artist C. Michael Lewis, but most eventually disappeared. In 1986 a memorial plaque was mounted on a boulder positioned on the site of the CCC Office at the left of the entrance to Portland Head Light.

The park is widely used by Greater Portland residents for athletics (particularly tennis), picnicing, and sightseeing. Various family and childrens' events are held in the park, as well as major events such as antique auto shows and the annual Portland Symphony Orchestra's 4th of July concert. In 1998 *The Beach To Beacon Race*, 3,000 participant world class running event, finished its 10K course at Fort Williams. The lighthouse has always been a popular tourist destination, ever increasing with many tour buses.

The opening of the museum at the lighthouse in 1992 created an additional attraction at this scenic location. One room in the museum is devoted to Fort Williams, and includes a large scale model of the fort, numerous photographs, and the enamel sign from Battery Garesche.

Organizational insignia: (Top to bottom, left to right) Harbor Defenses of Portland, Coast Artillery, 8th C.A, 68th C.A., 240th C.A., Infantry, 5th Infantry, C.C.C.

Bibliography and Further Reading Guide

Adams, David M., "A Military History of Fort Williams" (unpublished, 1975).

Army and Navy Publishing Co., *Historical and Pictorial Review, National Guard of the State of Maine, 1939* (Baton Rouge, 1939).

Army-Navy Publishers, Inc., *Pictorial History, Harbor Defenses of Boston, 1941* (Atlanta, 1941).

—*Pictorial History, Harbor Defenses of Portland, 1941* (Atlanta, 1941).

Bachelder, Peter Dow, *The Lighthouses and Lightships of Casco Bay* (Portland, 1995).

Barnes, Albert F., comp., *Greater Portland Celebration 350* (Portland, 1984).

Benoit, Peter W., *History of Jewell Island Maine* (Portland?, 1996).

Berry, Marcelia R., Miriam C. Chapman, Constance C. Murray, and Elizabeth B. Peterson, *Cape Elizabeth, Past to Present* (Cape Elizabeth, 1991).

Bogart, Charles H., *Controlled Mines, A History Of Their Use By The United States* (Bennington, Vermont, 1986).

Bradley, Robert L., *The Forts of Maine, 1607-1945: An Archaeological and Historical Survey* (Augusta, 1981).

Brandt, Elena, "Fort Williams, Cape Elizabeth, Me., A Review of the Current Situation and Recommendations for Future Action" (Portland, 1974)

Browning, Robert S. III, *The Development of American Coastal Defense Policy* (Westport, Connecticut, 1983).

Cape Elizabeth Advisory Committee, "A Report on the Feasibility of Having an Oceanographic Institute (TRIGOM) Locate On Fort Williams, Cape Elizabeth, Maine" (Cape Elizabeth, 1969).

— "Survey of the Thinking of Residents on the Development of Fort Williams" (Cape Elizabeth, 1970).

Cape Elizabeth Urban Renewal Authority, "Fort Williams Project [Map]" (James W. Sewall Company, 1965).

—"The Fort Williams Urban Renewal Project, A Report to the Citizens of Cape Elizabeth" (Cape Elizabeth, 1970).

Coast Defense Study Group News, vols. one-six, quarterly, 1985-1992.

—*Coast Defense Study Group Journal,* vols. 7-12, quarterly, 1993-present.

Comee, Edgar A., "The Bluff That Worked", *The Retired Officer* (October 1982), 30-31.

Conn, Stetson, Rose C. Engelman, and Byron Fairchild, *United States Army in World War II, The Western Hemisphere, Guarding the United States and its Outposts* (Washington, 1964).

Department of the Navy, Harbor Entrance Control Post, Fort Williams, "HECP, Portland History, November 1941 to June 1945".

—U. S. Naval Station, Portland, "U.S. Naval Station - Portland, Maine Administrative History", 1946.

Dwelley, Hugh L., "The mystery of Dirigible K-14", *Maine Journal,* vol. 1, no. 4

(May/June 1992), 13-15, 30.

Eastman, Joel W., "People: Pitching In", *Portland,* vol. IV, no. X (Winterguide 1990), 22-25, 28-29.

— "Portland At War, Deciphering Casco Bay's Elaborate Defense System", *Portland,* vol. 2, no. 6 (July-August 1987), 12-16, 22.

— "Temporary Buildings as Used at Coast Artillery Installations", *Coast Defense Study Group News,* vol. 4 (November 1990), no. 4, 22-24.

— "The Guns of Casco, Twentieth Century Fortifications Off Portland Harbor", *Island Journal,* vol. five (1987), 15-17.

— "The Modern Defenses of the Coast of Maine, 1891-1945", report prepared for the Maine Historic Preservation Commission, 1988.

— and James W. Flanagan, "Portlandiana: U-Boats off the Coast of Maine", *Portland,* vol. IV, no. X (Winterguide 1990), 14-15.

1st Battle Group, Fifth Infantry, *History of the Fifth United States Infantry* (Fort Riley, Kansas, 1960).

Flanagan, James W., "Fly Boys in the Blueberry Fields, The Making of BNAS, 1942", *Portland,* vol. IV, no. X (Winterguide 1990), 16-20.

— "NASB: Guarding the Maine Coasts", *Maine Journal,* vol. 1, no. 4 (May/June 1992), 22-26.

Floyd, Dale E., *Defending America's Coasts, 1775-1950, A Bibliography* (Washington, 1997).

Fort Williams Study Committee, "Report of the Fort Williams Study Committee" (Cape Elizabeth, 1976).

Goold, Nathan, *Falmouth Neck in the Revolution* (Portland, 1897).

Goold, William, *Portland In the Past* (Portland, 1886).

Grashof, Bethanie C., *A Study of United States Army Family Housing Standardized Plans,* 6 vols. (Atlanta, 1986).

Hawkes, Pamela, "Dignity and Desolation: Fort Williams, Cape Elizabeth, Maine" (unpublished, 1974).

Hayes, Thomas J., *Elements of Ordnance, A Textbook for Use of Cadets of the United States Military Academy* (New York, 1938).

Hines, Frank T. and Franklin W. Ward, *The Service of Coast Artillery* (New York, 1910).

Hoxie, Wilbar M., "Fortifications of Jewell Island, Portland Harbour, Maine", unpublished typescript in possession of the Maine Historical Society.

Johnson, Robert E., *Guardians of the Sea: History of the United States Coast Guard 1915 to the Present* (Annapolis, 1987).

Jolicouer, David, comp., "The Fort Williams Chronology, July 1963 to October 1995" (Cape Elizabeth, 1995).

Jones, Herbert G., *Portland Ships Are Good Ships* (Portland, 1945).

Jordan, William B. Jr., *A History of Cape Elizabeth, Maine* (Portland, 1965).

Kington, Donald M., *Forgotten Summers: The Story of the Citizens' Military Training Camps, 1921-1940* (San Francisco, 1995).

Lawry, Nelson H., "Book Review" [*The Casco Deception*], unpublished 1984.
—"Fields of Fire, Fort McKinley and the Defense of Great Diamond", *Island Journal,* vol. six (1989) , 64-67.
— "Fixed in Concrete: Sewell Construction Tactical Buildings 1906-1917", *Coast Defense Study Group Journal,* vol. 10 (November 1996), issue 4, 30-37.
—"Forts Fired Only One Shot In Anger ... and it missed", *Maine Sunday Telegram,* 5 March 1972.
—"The Kennebec Defended Through a Dozen Wars", *Periodical, Journal of the Council on America's Military Past,* vol. XIII (May 1985), no. 2, whole no. 51, 3-20.
Lewis, Emanuel Raymond, *Seacoast Fortifications of the United States: An Introductory History* (Washington, 1970).
Louda, Jiri and Michael Maclagan, *Lines of Succession, Heraldry of the Royal Families of Europe* (New York, 1991).
Maine, State of, *Report of the Adjutant General of the State of Maine for the Period of the World War 1917-1919* (Augusta, 1929), 2 vols.
—*The Official History of the Maine Civilian Defense Corps, 1941-1944* (Hallowell, 1945).
Malone, Danny, "Seacoast Artillery Radar 1938-46", *Coast Defense Study Group News,* vol. 3 (November 1989), no. 5, 1, 3-11.
McFarland, Earl, *Textbook of Ordnance and Gunnery* (New York, 1932).
McKinnon, Donna Lee, "Portland Defended, A History of the United States Government Fortifications of Casco Bay 1794-1945", unpublished Master's thesis, University of Maine, 1987.
Moffat, Alexander W., *A Navy Maverick Comes of Age, 1939-1945* (Middletown, 1977).
Newell, John R., *William Stark Newell (1878-1954), Shipbuilder of Maine* (New York,   1955)
Parkman, Aubrey, *Army Engineers in New England, The Military and Civil Work of the Corps of Engineers in New England, 1775-1975* (Waltham, 1978).
Polaski, Leo, "The Standard Endicott Period Fire Control, *Coast Defense Study Group New,* vol.3 (November 1988), no. 1, 8-9.
Porter, C. F., *A Brief History of the Works Erected for the Defense of Portland, Maine* (Washington, 1905).
Quinn, William P., *Shipwrecks Around Maine (Illustrated)* (Orleans, Massachusetts, 1983).
[Ray, Roger B.], *Cape Elizabeth and the American Revolution* (Cape Elizabeth, 1975).
The Research Institute of Maine, "Fort Williams Coastal Science Park" (1971).
Roerden, Chris, *Collections From Cape Elizabeth* (Cape Elizabeth, 1965).
Sarty, Roger F.., *Coast Artillery 1815-1914* (Alexandria Bay. New York, 1988).
Schlenker, Jon A., Norman A. Wetherington, and Austin H. Wilkins, *In the Public Interest, the civilian conservation corps in maine, A Pictorial History* (Au-

gusta, 1988).

Schroder, Walter K., *Defenses of Narragansett Bay in World War II* (East Greenwich, Rhode Island, 1980).

Smith, Bolling W., "Coast Artillery Companies, 1901-1919", *Coast Defense Study Group News,* vol.5 (May 1991). no. 2, 10-14.

—"Meteorological and Tide Stations, 1890-1917", *Coast Defense Study Group Journal,* vol. 11 (February 1997), issue 1, 23-36.

Smith, Mason Philip, *Confederates Downeast, Confederate Operations In And Around Maine* (Portland, 1985).

Snow, Ralph Linwood, *Bath Iron Works, The first hundred years* (Bath, 1987).

Sterling, Robert F., *Lighthouses of the Maine Coast and the Men Who Keep Them* (Brattleboro, 1935).

Taylor, Emerson Gifford, *New England in France 1917-1919, A History of the Twenty-Sixth Division U. S. A.* (Boston, 1920).

The Current, "Fort Williams, Our crumbling link to the past", June 16, 1981, 1, 4, 7, 10.

240th Coast Artillery Regiment, "History of the 240th Coast Artillery (Harbor Defenses of Portland)", unpublished typescript, [1941].

—"240th Coast Artillery (Harbor Defense) (First Maine) , One Hundred and Seventy Years", unpublished typescript for regimental officers' reunion, 1969.

—*240th Coast Artillery (Harbor Defense) Maine National Guard, History and Year Book, 1930* (Cape Elizabeth?, 1930).

—*240th Coast Artillery (Harbor Defense) Maine National Guard, Year Book 1935* (Cape Elizabeth?, 1935).

U. S. Army, Corps of Engineers, "Plan and Sections of a Battery for Portland Head, Maine" (April 1870) , National Archives Cartographic, RG 77, Drawer 10, Sheet 23.

—"Portland Harbor Showing site of Proposed Defences for Main Entrance" (August, September 1864) , National Archives Cartographic, RG 77, Drawer 10, Sheets 15a and 15B.

—"Portland Harbor, Maine, Diagram of Fields of Fire of Forts and proposed Batteries" (May 1870) , National Archives Cartographic, RG 77, Drawer 10, Sheet 21.

U. S. Army, Engineer Intelligence Division, Governors Island, N. Y., "Map of Fort Williams, Portland, ME" (September 1960).

U. S. Army, Engineer Office, Portland, Maine, "Plans of Batteries Proposed for defence of Portland Harbor" (January 1862), National Archives Cartographic, RG 77, Drawer 10 Sheet 14.

U. S. Army, Harbor Defenses of Portland, "History of the Harbor Defenses of Portland for the period 31 March 1944 to 31 December 1946", National Archives, RG 94.

U. S. Army, Office of the Construction Quartermaster, Fort Preble, "Sewer System, Map of Fort Williams, Maine" [mid 1941].

U. S. Army, Portland Subsector, "History Portland Subsector [11 December 1941 to 1 March 1944]", National Archives, RG 94.

U. S. Congress, *American State Papers, Military Affairs* (Washington, 1832-1860), vols. 1-6.

—Naval Affairs Committee, "[No. 118], Report on the Portland, Maine, Area by the Subcommittee of the Naval Affairs Committee Appointed to Investigate Congestion in Critical War Production Areas", 1943.

U. S. Navy, District Public Works Officer, "Map of U. S. Navy H. E. C. P., Fort Williams, Casco Bay, Maine" (June 30, 1945).

U. S. War Department, "Annexes to Harbor Defense Project, Harbor Defenses of Portland", 1915.

—"Annexes to Harbor Defense Project, Harbor Defenses of Portland", 1938.

—"Annexes to Harbor Defense Project, Harbor Defenses of Portland", 1945.

—"Basic Harbor Defense Project, Harbor Defenses of Portland", 1943.

—*Coast Artillery Weapons and Materiel, Technical Manual TM 4-210* (Washington, 1940).

—"Harbor Defense Projects for Harbor Defenses Included in the Portland-Cape Cod Area", 1932.

— Portland, Maine District Engineer, "Report of Completed Batteries, Etc. for December 31, 1907".

—Portland, Maine District Engineer, "Report of Completed Batteries, Etc. for December 31, 1910".

—Quartermaster Corps, Building Record Books, "Fort Levett", 'Fort Lyon", "Fort McKinley", and "Fort Preble", "QM Form No. 117", in possession of the South Portland-Cape Elizabeth Historical Society, South Portland.

—Quartermaster Corps, Building Record Books, "Fort Williams", "QM Form No.117", in possession of Cape Elizabeth Historical Society, Thomas Memorial Library, Cape Elizabeth.

—"Report of Completed Works - Seacoast Fortifications (Gun and Mortar Batteries)" for batteries Blair (1919,27), DeHart (1919,20,27), Garesche (1919, 20), Hobart (1929), Keyes (1919), Sullivan (1919, 20, 27), and 961 (1945).

Weaver, Robert A., "Heroism, for a Pigeon, Is Duck Soup!", *Periodical, Journal of the Council on America's Military Past,* vol. XVI (July 1989), no. 2, whole no. 63, 52-53.

Willis, William, *The History of Portland* (Portland, 1865).

Winslow, Eben Eveleth, *Notes on Seacoast Fortification* (Washington, 1920).

Wisser, John P., *The Tactics of Coast Defense* (Kansas City, 1902).

Zink, Robert D., "Controlled Submarine Mining in the United States", *Coast Defense Study Group Journal,* vol. 9 (November 1995), issue 4, 42-54.

—"The Forts of 'Wherever' #2, The Coast Defenses of Portland, Maine", *Coast Defense Study Group News,* vol. 3 (February 1989), no. 2, 9-13.

Index

Alexander, Charles A., 25
Army, British, 12
Army commands, U. S.:
  Antiaircraft Artillery Command, 88
  Artillery District of Portland, 33
  Eastern Defense Command, 71
  Eastern Theatre of Operations, 71
  Ellsworth Local Sector, 79
  Harbor Defenses of Portland, 62, 72, 75-76, 82, 84-85, 88, 93
  Harbor Defenses of Portsmouth (NH), 47, 63, 72-73, 82
  Maine Military District, 88-90
  Maine Sector, 90-91
  Military District, Maine, 90
  Northeast Defense Command, 71
  Northeast Frontier Defense Sector, 71-72
  Organized Reserve Corps (ORC), 88
  Portland Frontier Defense Sub-Sector, 72
  Portland Subsector, 72, 75, 79, 82, 84
  Portsmouth Local Sector (NH), 72, 79
  Rockland Local Sector, 79
Army units, U. S.:
  1st through 13th companies, CAC, Maine NG, 38, 41-42
  1st Coast Defense Command, Maine NG, 44
  1st Connecticut Infantry Regiment, 23
  1st Maine Infantry Regiment, 31, 37
  1st Massachusetts Heavy Artillery Regiment, 31
  2nd Artillery Regiment, 23
  5th Coast Artillery Company, 37
  5th Infantry Regiment, 49-51, 56-57, 93
  7th Artillery Regiment, 23
  8th Coast Artillery Regiment, 47, 51, 57, 59, 60, 62, 66, 72-73, 93
  9th Coast Artillery Company, 37
  9th Coast Artillery Regiment, 47
  10th Coast Artillery Regiment, 47
  22nd Coast Artillery Regiment, 72-73
  26th Division, 42
  49th Coast Artillery Company, 37
  51st Field Artillery Brigade, 42
  54th Coast Artillery Regiment, 42
  65th Ordnance Detachment, 90
  68th Coast Artillery Regiment, 58-59, 93
  72nd Coast Artillery Regiment, 42
  89th Coast Artillery Company, 37
  101st Engineers, 42
  101st Field Artillery Regiment, 42
  102nd Field Artillery Regiment, 42
  103rd Field Artillery Regiment, 42
  107th Coast Artillery Company, 37
  155th Coast Artillery Company, 37
  173d Medical Detachment, 90
  185th Coast Artillery Battalion, 85, 88
  186th Coast Artillery Battalion, 85, 88
  219th Antiaircraft Artillery Group, 88
  240th Antiaircraft Artillery Group, 88, 91
  240th Coast Artillery Regiment, 45, 47, 55, 59-60, 62-66, 68-69, 73, 75-76, 79, 85, 90 93
  302d Military Police Battalion, 90
  303d Army Postal Unit, 90
  417th Infantry Regiment, 90
  752d Transportation Company, 90
  901st Field Artillery Battalion, 90
  991st Signal Battalion, 90
  1033d ARASU, 90
  1033d ARSU, 90-91
  1033rd ORC, 90
  1074th Transportation Company, 90
  1104th Corps Area Service Unit, 63
  1128th ASU, 90
  1128th SU, 90
  Combat Team 81-2, 73, 84
Augusta, 23
Bailey Island (Casco Bay), 78-79, 82
Bald Head (Phippsburg), 54
Balloons, Observation, 46, 49, 64
Band, 28, 37, 50, 57, 85
Bar Harbor, 86
Bath Iron Works, 41, 72
Batteries, Gun:
  Alert, 68, 83
  AMTB #1, 82-83
  AMTB #4, 83

Antiaircraft, 42, 53, 82, 84
Anti-Motor Torpedo Boat (AMTB), 82, 84, 86
  at Bailey Island, 79, 82
  at Biddeford Pool, 73
  at Chebeague Island, 82
  at Drinkwater Point, 82
  at Fort Baldwin, 41, 72-73
  at Fort Levett, 37, 42, 80, 84
  at Fort Lyon, 37, 82
  at Fort McKinley, 37
  at Fort Preble, 36-37
  at Fort Williams, 8, 18-19, 22, 29-32, 42, 45, 52-53, 55, 64, 67, 70, 72, 75, 82-84, 92
  at Jewell Island, 80, 82, 84
  at Long Island, 82
  at Peaks Island, 80, 82, 84
  at Stockton Springs, 79
  at Two Lights, 80, 82, 84
  Blair, 19, 21, 29-30, 55-56, 64, 70-72, 75, 82-84
  Cravens, 84
  DeHart, 22, 29, 53, 75
  earthworks at Fort Preble, 13, 15
  earthworks at Fort Scammell, 13
  earthworks at Little Diamond Island, 15
  earthworks at Portland Head, 14-15, 89
  Foote, 42, 80, 84
  Garesche, 32, 42, 44-45, 52-53, 56, 59, 92
  Hobart, 29, 32, 35-36, 52
  Keyes, 31-32, 35, 40, 45, 54, 62, 64, 68, 83-84
  Steele, 80, 84
  Sullivan, 18, 22, 29, 36, 42, 53-54, 67, 84
  typical (generic), 20
  961, 82
Beach to Beacon Race, The, 92
Biddeford Pool, 73
Biological Survey, U. S., 56
Blair, Maj. Gen. Francis P., 29
Blimps:
  K-14, 86
  TC13, 60
Board of Engineers, U. S. Army, 13
Bowdoin College (Brunswick), 9, 79
Brunswick Naval Air Station (BNAS), 88
Buoy Station (Portland Harbor), 9
Bureau of Lighthouses, U. S., 5, 7-9
Camps, U. S. Army:
  Devens (MA), 41
  Edwards (MA), 59
  Keyes, 32
  Langdon (NH), 72
  Shelby (MS), 85
Cape Cottage (Cape Elizabeth), 8
Cape Cottage Park (Cape Elizabeth), 15-16, 26
Cape Elizabeth (headland), 2-3
Cape Elizabeth (town), 2-3, 5-6, 10, 15-16, 78, 80, 82, 91
Cape Porpoise (Kennebunkport), 80
Cape Small (Phippsburg), 54
Casco Bay, 2, 5-7, 12, 16, 18, 54, 69-70, 75, 77, 82-83, 87
Casco Bay Lines (Portland), 62
Casco Deception, The, 77
Castine, 12
Chandler Cove (Casco Bay), 70
Chebeague Island (Casco Bay), 82
Citizens' Military Training Camps (CMTC), 51
Civil Air Patrol, 78, 89
Civilian Conservation Corps (CCC), 56-57, 59, 92-93
Civilian Conservation Corps units:
  165th Company, 57
  1131st Company, 57
Coast Artillery Corps, U. S. Army, 37, 47, 62, 81, 88, 93
Coast Guard, U. S., 8-10, 77
Composite Task Force 69, U. S. Navy, 87
Corbett, Glenn, 91
Corps of Engineers, U. S. Army, 13, 15
Cow Island (Casco Bay), 18, 36
Crescent Beach (Cape Elizabeth), 32
Cushing Island (Casco Bay), 3, 18, 36, 80
Cushing Point (South Portland), 67
Daboll Trumpet, 6, 8
Damariscotta, 73

Davis, Bette, 82
Dearborn, Sec. of War Henry, 12
De Hart, Capt. Henry V., 22-23
Delano, Barzillai, 8
Delano, James, 9
Dimout Program, 9, 77
Doenitz, Grand Adm. Karl, 87
Drinkwater Passage (Casco Bay), 70
Drinkwater Point (Yarmouth), 82
Dyer's Cove (Cape Elizabeth), 5, 9
Eastern Cemetery (Portland), 12
Eastport, 12, 66
Elizabeth, Queen of Bohemia, 2
Ellsworth, 79
Endicott Board, U. S. Army, 17
Falmouth, 2-3, 16
Falmouth Harbor, 3
Feeney, John M., 16
Field Artillery Corps, U. S. Army, 37, 79, 90
Fire Control Systems:
    Base-end stations, 31-33, 36-37, 77-78, 80
    Coincidence Range Finder (CRF), 31, 40, 45
    Depression Position Finder, 30
    Gunner's skill, 30
    Horizontal Base Line, 31, 36, 45
    Self-contained, horizontal base, range finder, 31, 45
    Vertical position finding, 30
Fires, 53-54
Fogg, Brig. Gen. George E., 79, 91
Ford, John, 16
Forest Service, Maine, 56
Forest Service, U. S., 56
Fort Williams study committees:
    Citizens Advisory Committee, 91
    Fort Williams Advisory Commission, 91
    Fort Williams Advisory Committee, 91
    Fort Williams Improvement Committee, 91
    Fort Williams Planning Committee, 91
    Fort Williams Study Committee, 91
    Urban Renewal Authority, 91
Fort Williams Park, 91-92

Forts:
    Allen, 4, 12
    at Portland Head (proposed), 14
    at Spring Point, 3
    Baldwin, 41, 72, 80, 84, 89
    Burrows, 4, 12
    Constitution (NH), 72
    Foster, 72
    Gorges, 4, 13-15
    Hancock, 3, 12
    Jackson (SC), 85
    Lawrence, 4, 12
    Levett, 4, 36, 41-42, 47, 59, 63-64, 79-80, 82, 89-90
    Lyon, 4, 36-37, 47, 82, 88
    McKinley, 4, 36-38, 41, 46-47, 50-51, 58, 60, 62-63, 66, 69, 75, 89
    Monmouth (NJ), 47
    Preble, 4, 12-15, 18, 22-23, 33, 36-37, 39, 41, 47, 50, 53-54, 60, 62, 72, 82, 88-90
    Pulaski (GA), 14
    Scammel, 12
    Scammell, 4, 12-14
    Stark (NH), 72
    Sumner, 4, 11
    Warren (MA), 14
    Williams, 1, 4, 8-10, 23-92
    Worden (WA), 46
    H. G. Wright (NY), 58
Freeman, Joshua, 8
Fresnel lens, 6, 8-9
Garesché, Lt. Col. Julius P., 32
Garrett, Brig. Gen. Robert C., 58, 62
Gere, Richard, 47
Goddard, Col. John, 25-26
Goddard Mansion, 16, 25-26, 28, 60, 62
Gorham, 66
Gossett, Louis Jr., 47
Grant, Gen. Ulysses S., 23
Great Diamond Island (Casco Bay), 18, 36, 69
Gulf of Maine, 78
Gun Mounts:
    Balanced Pillar, 21

Barbette, 21
Disappearing Carriage, 19, 21-22, 29, 32
Masking Parapet, 21
Mobile, 55, 73, 75, 84
Panama, 73
Pedestal, 21, 29, 32
Guns:
  Antiaircraft, 42, 44, 53-54, 73, 75, 82, 84
  Armstrong, 29-30
  Breechloading, 22, 29, 32
  GPF, 54-55, 63, 67, 72-73, 79, 83
  Intermediate, 21
  Mortars, 18, 36-37
  Primary, 21
  Quick-Firing, 22, 29
  Range of, 22, 30, 32, 42, 55, 73, 80, 82
  Rapid-Fire, 21-22, 32, 82
  Rifled, 14
  Salute, 65, 76
  Secondary, 21
  Smoothbore, 14
  3-inch, 18, 21, 32, 37, 41-42, 53-54, 73, 75, 82, 84-85
  4.72-inch, 21
  6-inch, 18, 21, 29-30, 32, 36-37, 41-42, 80, 84-85
  8-inch, 18-19, 21, 37
  10-inch, 18, 22, 37, 42, 45
  12-inch, 18-19, 29-30, 37, 42, 64
  12-inch mortars, 18, 21, 36-37
  16-inch, 80, 84
  30-caliber machine gun, 68, 82
  37-mm., 82
  50-caliber machine gun, 54
  57-mm., 89
  75-mm., 89
  90-mm., 82
  155-mm., 54-55, 63, 67, 72-73, 79, 83
Guthrie, Arlo, 70
Guthrie, Woody, 70
Hancock, 86
Harbor Defense Command Post (HDCP), 53, 74-75, 84
Harbor Entrance Control Post (HECP), 68, 70, 74-76

Hathaway, George M., 11
Heywood, Maj. Gen. Edwin W., 90-91
Hobart, 1st Lt. Henry A., 29
Hog Island Ledge (Casco Bay), 13
Holmes, Brig. Gen. Alonzo B., 79
Holt, Harrison J., 29
Homing pigeons, 47
Hopper, Edward, 11
House Island (Casco Bay), 9, 12-13
Hussey Sound (Casco Bay), 14, 32, 37, 70, 75, 87
Infantry, U. S. Army, 47, 50, 93
Jewell Island (Casco Bay), 4, 80, 82, 84, 89
Jones, Brig. Gen. Thomas H., 79, 84
Kennebec River, 41, 72-73, 80, 84
Keyes, Maj. Gen. Erasmus D., 32
Kimball, Sumner I., 9
Kittery, 87
Large Navigational Buoy (LNB), 6
Lee, Vice Adm. Willis A. Jr., 87
Lewis, C. Michael, 92
Liberty Ships, 67-68
Life-Saving Service, U. S., 9
Life-Saving Station (Cape Elizabeth), 9, 77
Lighthouse, The, (poem), 1
Lighthouse Board, U. S., 7-8
Lighthouses:
  Breakwater Light, 4, 6
  Bug Light, 4, 6
  Cape Elizabeth Lights, 4-5, 9, 80
  Halfway Rock Light, 6
  Portland Head Light, 1, 3-12, 14-15, 22, 29, 33, 44, 55-56, 59, 67, 73, 77, 83, 87, 92
  Ram Island Ledge Light, 4, 6
  Spring Point Ledge Light, 4, 6
  Two Lights, 6
Lightships:
  Cape Elizabeth, 6
  Portland, 6
Little Chebeague Island (Casco Bay), 69
Little Diamond Island (Casco Bay), 9, 15
Littlejohn Passage (Casco Bay), 70, 87
Long Island (Casco Bay), 69, 82
Longfellow, Henry W., 1

Loomis, Brig. Gen. Harold F., 72, 79
Machias, 75
Maine Stein Song, 50
Medical Corps, U. S. Army, 37, 50, 53, 56, 63, 90
Merrill, Gary, 82
Meteorological Station, 31, 33, 75
Midnight at Mears House, 29
Military Reservations:
   Cape Elizabeth, 4, 80, 82, 84, 89
   Jewell Island, 4, 80, 82, 84, 89
   Peaks Island, 4, 80, 82, 84, 89
Milk Street Armory (Portland), 45
Milner, Martin, 91
Mines:
   Buoyant mines, 17-18, 33, 35, 53, 70, 82, 87
   Electrical submarine mines, 17-18, 33, 35, 53
   Mine Control Observation Stations, 35-36, 89
   Mine Planting, 18, 33, 35, 53
   Mine assembly, 33, 37
   Mine Wharf, 33, 35, 53
   Mining Casemate, 17-18, 33, 37
   Mining Tramway, 33, 35, 53
Modernization Program, 80, 84, 89
Morris, George W., 11
Mount Agamenticus (York), 54
Mowatt, Capt. Henry, 3
Munjoy Hill (Portland), 1, 11-12
Museum At Portland Head Light, The, 10, 92
National Liberty Ship Memorial. 68
National Park Service, U. S., 56
National Register of Historic Places, 10
Naval Air Station Brunswick (NASB), U.S., 82, 88
Naval Reserve Training Center, U. S. (South Portland), 91
Naval Station Portland, U. S., 69, 88
Navy:
   British, 3, 12. 69, 82
   Confederate States, 14
   German, 8, 42, 84
   Spanish, 8
   United States, 9, 60, 68-70, 75-78, 86-87
Nixon, President Richard M., 17
Normandy Invasion, 68, 86
North Africa Invasion, 82
Nurses, U. S. Army, 62-63
Officer and a Gentleman, An, 47
Peaks Island (Casco Bay), 30, 80, 82-84, 89
Pemaquid, 12
Penobscot River, 79
Popham Beach (Phippsburg), 72, 89
Portland, 1-3, 6, 10-14, 16-17, 50, 57, 60, 66-67, 69, 76, 78-79, 86, 90
Portland Airport, 60, 78
Portland Harbor, 1-3, 9-14, 17-18, 22, 31, 41-42, 49, 59, 62, 66-67, 70, 72, 75-76, 79-80, 82, 84-86, 88, 93
Portland Head (Cape Elizabeth), 1-3, 5-6, 8, 12-18, 22-23, 36, 91
Portland Island (Casco Bay), 3
Portland Pipe Line, 67, 69
Portland Point (Cape Elizabeth), 2-3
Portland Press Herald, 66, 70
Portland Sound (Casco Bay), 2-3, 12, 32, 76
Portland Symphony Orchestra, 92
Portsmouth Naval Base (Kittery), 87
Postal Service, U. S., 11
Postcards, 11
Quartermaster Corps, U. S. Army, 25-26. 37, 40, 50, 56, 63-64
Radar Station, 83
Radio Station, 53
Ram Island Ledge (Casco Bay), 6
Read, Lt. Charles W., 14
Redbank (South Portland), 68
Reiss, Bob, 77
Revenue Cutter Service, U. S., 9, 14
Riverton Park (Portland), 16
Rockland-Vinalhaven Steamboat Company, 62
Route 66, 91
Saco, 73, 84
Sagamore Village (Portland), 68
Scammell, Col. Alexander, 12
Searchlight, Disappearing, 40, 45-47, 49

Searchlights, 40, 45-47, 49, 59, 64, 68, 83
Searsport, 79
Sewell, Capt. John S., 36
Shatner, William, 91
Ship Cove (Casco Bay), 17-18, 33-35, 53
Shipyards, 67-68
Signal Corps, U. S. Army, 47
Signal Station, 53
Smith, Capt. John, 2
South Portland, 3, 9, 15, 67, 91
Spring Point (South Portland), 3, 6, 13, 67
Spring Point Ledge (Casco Bay), 6
Stanford's Point (South Portland), 6
Star Trek, 91
Stockton Springs, 79
Strout, Joseph W., 9
Strout, Joshua, 9
Strout, Mary, 9
Sullivan, Maj. Gen. John, 22
Tide Station, 31, 33, 75
Titanic (movie), 68
Topsham, 79
Trolley parks, 15-16
Two Lights (Cape Elizabeth), 4, 6, 77, 80, 84, 89
Two Lights State Park, 76, 80
U-boats, 57, 69, 78, 86-87
Underwood Springs (Falmouth), 16
Union Mutual Insurance Company (UNUM), 92
Vessels:
  Alabama, 86
  Annie C. Maguire, 7-8
  Arkansas, 86
  Aucocisco, 62
  Blairlogie, 57
  Boxer, 12
  Caleb Cushing, 14
  Cantigny, 49-50
  Denebola, 70
  Eagle 56, 87
  Enterprise, 12
  Green Island, 62
  Indiana, 86
  Iowa, 86
  Jeremiah O'Brien, 68
  John F. Kennedy, 10
  Massachusetts, 86
  Nevada, 86
  New Jersey, 86
  New York, 86
  North Carolina, 86
  North Haven, 62
  Oakey L. Alexander, 76
  Ocean, 67
  Queen Elizabeth 2, 10
  Reuben James, 69
  South Dakota, 86
  Texas, 86
  Titanic, 68
  U-562, 69
  U-853, 87
  U-1230, 86
Wars:
  American Revolution, 3, 12
  Civil War, 9, 13-14, 32
  Korean War, 89
  Spanish-American War, 8, 22
  War of 1812, 12
  World War I, 8, 11, 16, 41, 72, 79, 84, 88
  World War II, 31, 40, 47, 57-87
Washington, President George, 5
Watertown Arsenal (MA), 41
Wayne, John, 17
Whitehead Passage (Casco Bay), 70
Williams, Daniel, 23
Williams, Gov. Joseph H., 23
Williams, Sen. Reuel, 23
Williams, Bvt. Maj. Gen. Seth, 23
Winter Harbor, 60
Women's Army Corps (WAC), 60